STEVE PARISH

AMAZING FACTS

ABOUT AUSTRALIAN

INSECTS & SPIDERS

AND OTHER BUSH AND GARDEN CREATURES

Text: Pat Slater

DISCOVER & LEARN • VOLUME 5

Contents

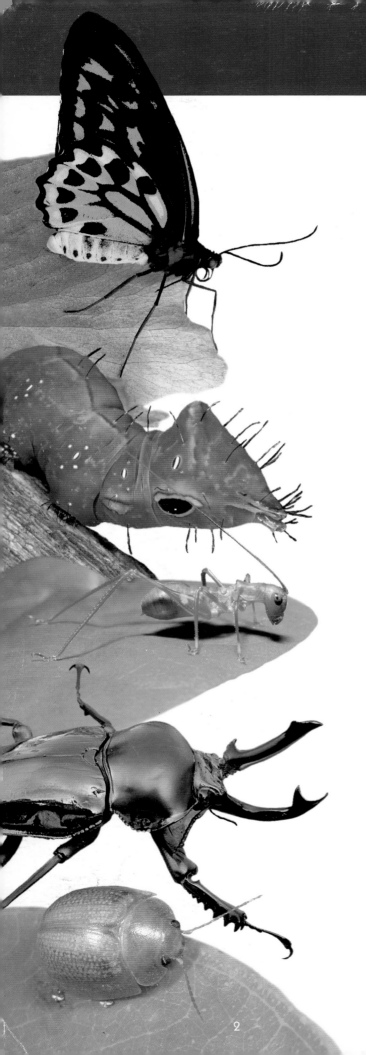

The fascinating invertebrates

A flower spider and its prey, an Orchard Swallowtail Butterfly

The Desert Green Ant lives in Western Australia's Great Sandy Desert

The above-ground section of a termite nest in Australia's north

The animal kingdom is divided by scientists into two major groups, the vertebrates (animals with backbones) and the invertebrates (animals without backbones).

Humans and other mammals*, birds, reptiles, fish and amphibians* belong in the group of vertebrates, which accounts for only around five per cent of earth's animal life.

The invertebrates which make up the other 95 per cent of animals include creatures of all sizes, shapes and lifestyles. An invertebrate may be a minute single-celled animal which lives in the bloodstream of another, larger animal. It may be a centipede, or a snail, or a shrimp, or an ant, or a giant squid with tentacles as long as a city bus.

Many land invertebrates, such as earthworms, spiders and a huge number of insects, affect human existence for better or for worse every day. Some invertebrates occupy human homes and gardens; some live on (and in) domestic animals. Many take a share of the crops humans grow for their own use. Some invertebrates, such as oysters, grasshoppers, snails and crabs, are eaten by humans.

This volume attempts to convey the diversity and fascination of the invertebrates which live in every Australian habitat*, from rainforest to desert salt lake, from mountain peak to suburban home. Look closely and you will discover that these small creatures are not "creepy-crawlies", but marvellous members of the great world of living things.

A katydid acts as courier for pollen

This spider-hunting wasp will lay an egg on the paralysed victim it is about to drag into its burrow

A leech waiting on foliage for a host

About this book

This book is intended to be an observer's introduction to Australia's wealth of land and freshwater invertebrate animals. The photographs showcase representatives of less well-known, as well as familiar, groups.

The Index inside the back cover will give ready reference to the creatures pictured. Look for words marked with an asterisk (*) in the Glossary on page 79. Some further reading is listed on page 80, and you may wish to visit your local library if you need to consult other reference books.

Welcome to a world of often small, but always remarkable, creatures!

The alien-from-space face of a Spotted Wattle Longicorn Beetle

The Marron, a freshwater cray, is farmed for human food

Invertebrates are a food source for many other animals

How animals are named

Common names and scientific names

Taxonomists are people who describe, identify and name living organisms. Worldwide, around two million animals and plants have been given scientific names by taxonomists so far.

With a few possible exceptions, every animal in this book has a scientific name. It may have a common name as well, but this will vary from place to place and language to language, whereas a scientific name will remain the same in all cultures and places.

So a Canadian, or an American, might look at an orange, black and white insect and call it a Monarch

Wanderer (or Monarch) Butterfly *Danaus plexippus*

Butterfly. An Australian might call the same insect a Wanderer Butterfly. They would be using their local common name for one animal, and any of them (or a Russian, Patagonian or Italian butterfly enthusiast) would give the insect the same scientific name — *Danaus plexippus*.

Classifying animals into groups

A species* is a group of similar animals which can breed with each other and produce fertile* offspring. The scientific name of a species consists of two words, always written in italics. The first word, the genus*, which places the animal in a group of very similar animals, is written with a capital initial letter. The second word, the species, which belongs only to that particular animal, is always written with a lower case initial letter. If a second reference is made to the same genus, the genus is represented by its initial letter only.

Taxonomists group animals with characteristics in common:

- A **kingdom** is made up of phyla.
- A **phylum** is made up of classes.
- A **class** is made up of orders.
- An **order** is made up of families.
- A **family** is made up of genera.
- A **genus** is made up of species.

Classification of Cairns Birdwing Butterfly
　　　　Kingdom: Animalia
　　　　　　Phylum: Arthropoda
　　　　　　　　Class: Insecta
　　　　　　　　　　Order: Lepidoptera
　　　　　　　　　　　　Family: Papilionidae
　　　　　　　　　　　　　　Genus: *Troides*
　　　　　　　　　　　　　　　　Species: *T. priamus*

Note: In this book, the common name of a species is given capitals, e.g., Sydney Funnel-web Spider.
When referring to groups of animals, lower case initials are used, e.g., the funnel-web spiders.

The greater part of the animal kingdom

This book deals with invertebrates which live on dry land or in fresh water. (Marine invertebrates feature in another volume in this series.)

By far the greatest number of invertebrates, including insects, spiders, crabs, millipedes and centipedes, belong to a division of the animal kingdom called the arthropods (Phylum Arthropoda).

All arthropods have the following characteristics in common:

- a hard external skeleton (termed an exoskeleton)
- a segmented body, with groups of segments organised into working parts, e.g., thorax, abdomen
- jointed limbs

THE IMPORTANCE OF THE ARTHROPODS IN THE ANIMAL KINGDOM

The chart shows the relative number of species in each of the major groups of animals.

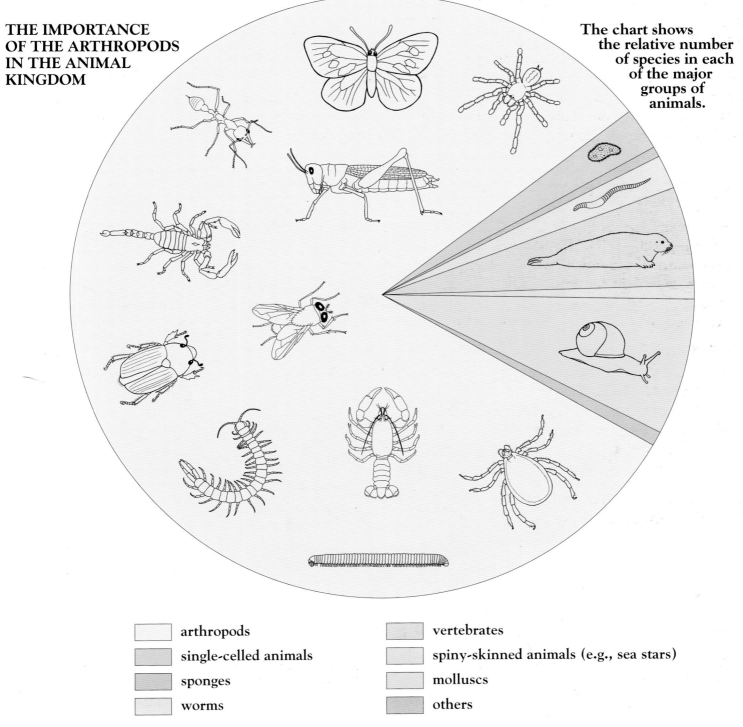

☐ arthropods		☐ vertebrates	
☐ single-celled animals		☐ spiny-skinned animals (e.g., sea stars)	
☐ sponges		☐ molluscs	
☐ worms		☐ others	

DID YOU KNOW?

FACTS

- Fossils are the preserved remains, or traces, of plants or animals from past ages. Minerals may replace the original body parts, or a cast of the organism (or its footprints) may remain preserved in rock.

- A small animal such as an insect may be preserved in fossilised tree sap (amber).

- The first true insect fossils come from the Carboniferous period, around 300 million years ago. Some of these were huge, dragonfly-like creatures with wingspans of up to 75 cm.

- The earliest primitive insects probably looked rather like the silverfish of today.

- The first insect-like fossils have been found in Devonian rocks over 350 million years old.

- Fossil velvet worms, little different from present-day forms, have been found in Cambrian rocks as old as 550 million years. (See p. 75 for more on today's velvet worms.)

A timeline for life on Earth

	vertebrates	invertebrates	
PRESENT **QUATERNARY** 2 million years ago	The rise of humans.		
TERTIARY 65 million years ago	Mammals dominant. Dinosaurs extinct.	Most of today's orders of insects in existence.	
CRETACEOUS 145 million years ago		Development of modern spiders. Insect pollinators follow great development of flowering plants.	
JURASSIC 208 million years ago	Birds appear. True mammals appear.	Spiders expand their use of silk.	
TRIASSIC 245 million years ago	Mammal-like reptiles. Reptiles dominant.		
PERMIAN 280 million years ago	Reptiles diversify as amphibians decline.	Spiders follow insects into trees. Insects with larval and pupal stages in life histories appear. Insects which eat leaves appear.	
CARBONIFEROUS 355 million years ago	First reptiles.	Winged insects which eat seeds and suck plant juices appear. Spiders, scorpions and at least 11 orders of insects exist.	
DEVONIAN 408 million years ago	Amphibians emerge on land. Lungfish breathe free air.	Primitive* wingless insect-like arthropods, which eat dead plants.	
SILURIAN 438 million years ago	Fishes with jaws and armour-like scales.	Scorpion-like arthropods invade the land. Plants grow on land.	
ORDOVICIAN 510 million years ago	Jawless fishes. First marine vertebrates.	Corals. Molluscs.	
CAMBRIAN 540 million years ago		Complex marine invertebrates with hard exoskeletons (echinoderms*, trilobites*). Early sponges. Worms.	
550 million years ago		Single-celled marine animals with hard skeletons.	
590 million years ago		Soft-bodied, many-celled animals exist in the sea.	
PRECAMBRIAN			
2100 million years ago		First cells with nuclei* and complex structure.	
3500 million years ago		Oldest recorded life on Earth.	

What is an insect?

An insect is an invertebrate whose body is encased in, and supported by, an exoskeleton made up of separate pieces of hard material joined together by flexible lines. Like other arthropods, a growing insect must moult* its exoskeleton at intervals.

The body of an insect is divided into three pieces: head, thorax and abdomen.

The head carries one pair of antennae*, one pair of compound* eyes, up to three simple eyes, and mouthparts suited to the insect's way of life (usually for piercing, sucking or chewing).

The thorax is made up of three segments, each carrying one pair of jointed legs. In adult insects, the second and third segments may carry wings, varying in size and effectiveness between species.

The abdomen is composed of up to 11 segments. The tip may be adapted for use in mating, or as a sensory organ, or it may carry a sting, which is used for offence and defence.

The abdomens of some female insects end in ovipositors*, used for placing their eggs deeply in soil, or into plant or animal tissue.

A cicada displays membranous wings

This female cricket bears a long ovipositor

THE PARTS OF AN INSECT BODY

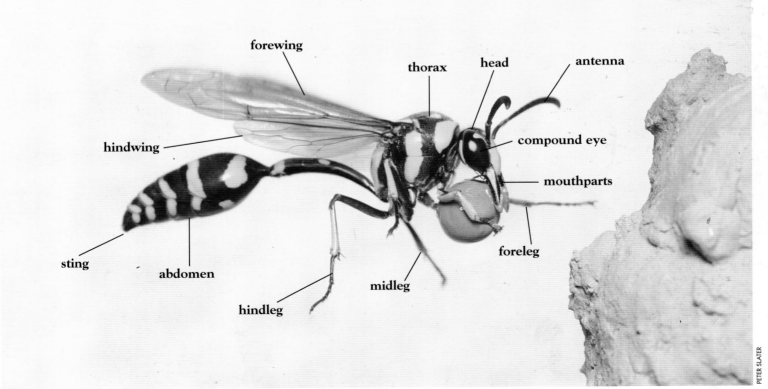

forewing
thorax
head
antenna
hindwing
compound eye
mouthparts
sting
abdomen
foreleg
hindleg
midleg

A mud-dauber wasp carrying a ball of mud to add to its nest

9

NAME OF ORDER	MEANING OF NAME	EXAMPLES	NUMBER OF SPECIES	
			WORLDWIDE	AUSTRALIA
Thysanura	bristle tails	silverfish	370	28
Ephemeroptera	brief-lived	mayflies	2500	84
Odonata	flies with teeth	dragonflies, damselflies	5000	302
Plecoptera	folded wings	stoneflies	2000	196
Blattodea	light-avoiders	cockroaches	4000	428
Isoptera	equal wings	termites	2300	348
Mantodea	like a prophet	mantids	1800	162
Dermaptera	leathery wings	earwigs	1800	63
Orthoptera	straight wings	grasshoppers, crickets	20 000	2827
Phasmatodea	like a ghost	phasmids (stick insects)	2000	150
Psocoptera	flour-dweller's wings	book lice, bark lice	3000	300
Phthiraptera	louse wings	parasitic* lice	3000	255
Hemiptera	half wings	includes bugs, aphids, cicadas	60 000	5650
Thysanoptera	fringed wings	thrips	4500	420
Megaloptera	great wings	alderflies, Dobsonflies	300	26
Neuroptera	net-veined wings	lacewings, ant-lions	5000	623
Coleoptera	sheath wings	includes beetles, weevils	>300 000	>28 200
Mecoptera	long wings	scorpion-flies	500	27
Siphonaptera	tube without wings	fleas	2380	90
Diptera	two wings	includes true flies, mosquitoes	150 000	7786
Trichoptera	hairy wings	caddis-flies	7000	480
Lepidoptera	scaly wings	moths, butterflies	100 000	20 816
Hymenoptera	membrane wings	includes ants, bees, wasps	>100 000	14 781

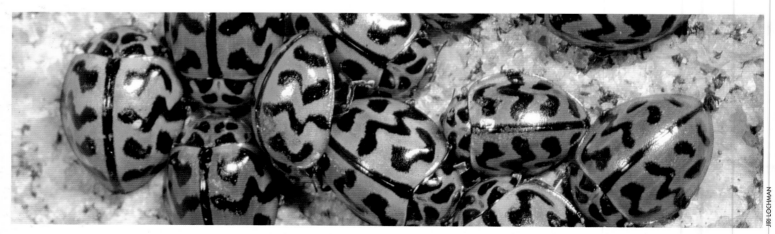

INSECT LIFE CYCLES

Some insects, such as silverfish, show **NO CHANGE** *throughout their lifetimes. They simply grow larger.*

Other insects, such as bugs, go through **GRADUAL CHANGES**. *Each young stage, or nymph*, is slightly more developed than the last. Wings, which begin as buds on the backs of hatchlings, are larger after each moult.*

Moths are typical of insects which go through a number of **ABRUPT CHANGES** *as they mature: egg, larva*, pupa* (or chrysalis) and adult. The wings develop inside the body and are seen only after the adult emerges from the pupal stage.*

NO CHANGE

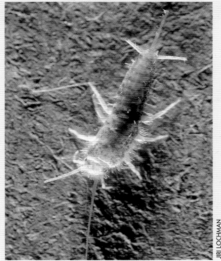

A silverfish grows larger without changing its shape

GRADUAL CHANGES

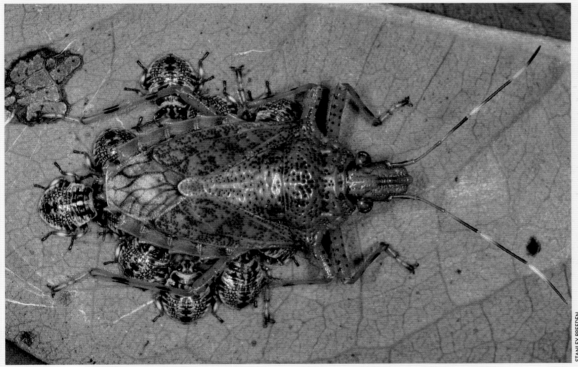

These young bugs will go through gradual changes, such as growing larger wings, as they mature

SERIES OF ABRUPT CHANGES

Emperor Gum Moth larva (above) will change to a pupa (not shown)

... from which will emerge the adult (above)

FACTS

▶ There are about 1 000 000 species of insects known to science – about 80% of all animals.

▶ One locust swarm was estimated to contain 40 000 million individuals.

▶ Each growth stage, between moults, of an arthropod (including insects) is called an instar*.

▶ An insect's compound eyes are made up of many six-sided lenses. A dragonfly may have more than 20 000 lenses in each eye.

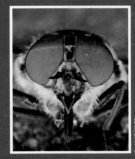

Eyes of March fly

▶ For a compound eye to see as well as a single-lens human eye does at a distance, it would have to be about 1 m across.

11

Winged insects escape by flying away

PETER SLATER

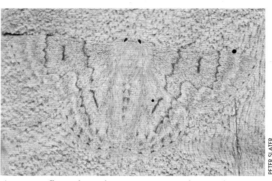

A camouflaged moth may escape a hunter's eye

PETER SLATER

An earwig defends itself with pincers

ERIC LINDGREN

A phasmid nymph regrowing a foreleg

STANLEY BREEDEN

Avoiding being eaten

Many animals, ranging from other insects to frogs, birds, reptiles and mammals, find insects good eating, so insects have developed many defences against attack.

Some insects have strong jaws or pincers. Others have long legs or efficient wings and simply run or fly away from danger. Certain insects produce chemicals which make them smell or taste nasty, or make their bodies poisonous. Some can squirt harmful chemicals some distance. Groups such as bees and wasps have venomous stings, while other groups such as beetles have powerful jaws. These may wear warning colours, while other, defenceless insects may be coloured to camouflage* them from predators*.

A damaged insect may be able to regrow injured limbs or antennae.

This grasshopper wears warning coloration

STEVE PARISH

A Banksia Moth caterpillar's threat display

JIRI LOCHMAN

Even newly hatched stink bugs smell nasty

JIRI LOCHMAN

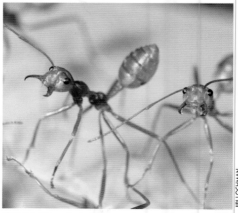

Green Tree Ants bite and spray formic acid

JIRI LOCHMAN

Changing skins

The outer skin, or cuticle*, of an insect cannot grow. As the insect gets larger, the cuticle must be shed, or moulted, from time to time.

Glands below the cuticle produce liquids that eat away the inner layer of the old cuticle, so a space appears between this layer and the new skin forming underneath. Finally, the old cuticle splits and the insect emerges. The new cuticle is soft, wrinkled and colourless until the insect pumps air into its body. Then the skin smoothes out and takes on colour. In many insects, its outer layer hardens.

Often the insect eats its moulted skin, though in some cases it provides a protective layer for the pupa.

IAN MORRIS

This bush cricket has just moulted

CROSS-SECTIONS OF INSECT BODIES

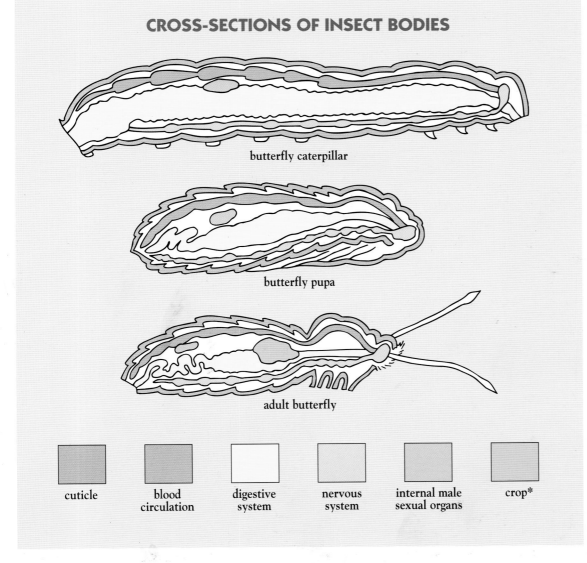

butterfly caterpillar

butterfly pupa

adult butterfly

- cuticle
- blood circulation
- digestive system
- nervous system
- internal male sexual organs
- crop*

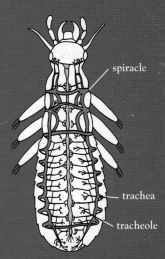

spiracle

trachea

tracheole

Air passes into an insect's body through openings called spiracles. The air may simply drift in, or be drawn in by pumping movements of the abdomen. It then diffuses through a network of fine tubes called tracheae and even finer branches called tracheoles.

13

The parasites

Many sorts of larval or adult insects feed on other animals. These parasites* may lay their eggs on, or in, the tissues of the host, or even in the host's eggs.

Some parasites, such as the larvae of horse bot-flies, are small in comparison to their hosts and harm them only if present in large numbers. Others, like the wasps whose larvae feed on caterpillars, entirely devour their hosts. The minute parasitic wasp crawling near the eye of the weevil at right lays its eggs inside the eggs of its host.

An egg parasite wasp crawls near the eye of a Wattle Pig Weevil from the Great Victoria Desert

Flies lay their eggs in food sources including rotting vegetation, carrion and living flesh

An Oak Blue Butterfly caterpillar attended by ants. The association benefits both parties. The ants protect the caterpillar and feed on sweet liquid it produces

This male flower wasp carries a wingless female wasp, mating with her as she feeds on nectar

Co-operative societies

Many species of insects gather together because they are attracted to a common source of food. However, ants, termites and some species of bees and wasps live in colonies*. In one colony there will be a number of different castes*, or groups which carry out different functions. These co-operative social insects gain strength from their numbers and are able to provide for their young with maximum efficiency.

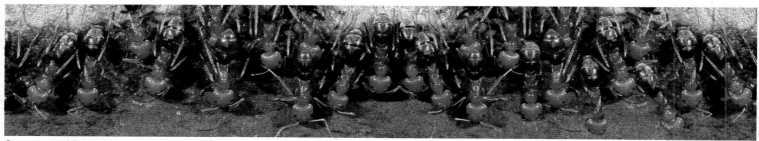

Sugar ants drinking. These and many other species of ants live in efficient co-operative societies

Mating Eucalyptus Leaf Beetles

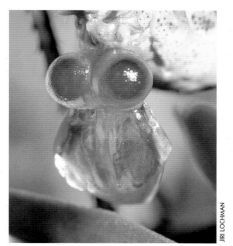
Spermatophore of a katydid

Making more insects

Male and female insects may be attracted to possible mates by sight, by scent or by sound. Once male and female make contact, the male usually places sperm*, or a package of sperm called a spermatophore*, inside the female's body through her reproductive opening in order to fertilise her eggs. Some female insects, for example phasmids and aphids, can produce fertile eggs without mating.

A praying mantid devouring an ambushed katydid

A sucking bug eating a caterpillar

A dragonfly consuming prey it has caught in flight

The predators

Insect hunters usually have strong legs and powerful jaws. Like dragonflies they may pursue prey in flight; like some beetles and bugs they may hunt on foot, or like praying mantids they may lurk in ambush, pouncing when a suitable victim appears.

DID YOU KNOW?

FACTS

▶ Butterflies and moths are classed together in the order Lepidoptera, meaning "scaly wings".

▶ There are more than 100 000 Lepidoptera species world wide. Of the 20 816 Australian species, only about 400 are butterflies.

▶ A caterpillar's first meal may be its own egg case. After that, most will eat only the plant on which their mother chose to lay her eggs. Some caterpillars eat other insects.

▶ Most adult butterflies feed on nectar and other liquids. A few do not eat at all.

▶ A caterpillar's false legs end in rings of tiny hooks.

▶ Australia's largest butterfly, the Cape York Birdwing, has a wingspan up to 14 cm.

▶ The world's largest butterfly, Queen Alexandra's Birdwing, which may measure 28 cm across the wings, lives in New Guinea. It flies so high that the first specimen collected was brought down with a shotgun blast.

Winged beauty

A butterfly's wings and body are covered by tiny overlapping scales, often brightly coloured and patterned. Part of the adult insect's mouthparts form a long, coiled tube, which is used for sucking up liquid.

The eyes are large and compound. The antennae are long, slender and often end in club-like swellings. There are two pairs of wings. Most butterflies rest with their wings held upright over their bodies. A butterfly larva, or caterpillar, has chewing mouthparts, three pairs of true legs on the thorax, and pairs of fleshy false legs on the abdomen.

PETER SLATER

The Cairns Birdwing is found from just north of Cooktown to Mackay, Qld

PETER MARSACK

A caterpillar of the large Cape York Birdwing Butterfly

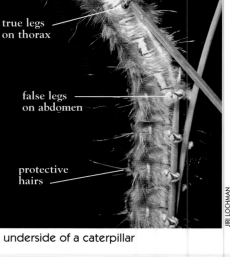

head
chewing mouthparts
true legs on thorax
false legs on abdomen
protective hairs

JIRI LOCHMAN

The underside of a caterpillar

LIFE HISTORY OF THE WANDERER BUTTERFLY

PETER MARSACK

A newly hatched caterpillar crawls away from its egg case

PETER MARSACK

The caterpillar feeds on poisonous milkweed and wears warning colours

It becomes a pupa, hanging fro a silk pad woven onto a twig

Flutter by, butterfly

Scales serve to strengthen a butterfly's wings and to act as signals to other butterflies.

Each has a stalk which fits into a tiny socket in the wing and the rows of scales overlap like tiles on a roof. Often the scales are coloured by pigments*. Their surfaces may be covered with ridges or lines, which break up light rays and produce iridescence*. The wings of the males of some species have special scent-scales, which send into the air odours used to attract females.

Scales and veins on wing of Imperial White Butterfly

PETER MARSACK

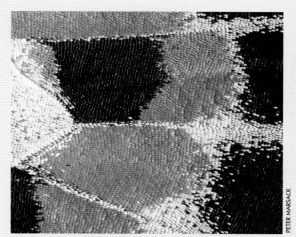
Australian Admiral wing displays hairs and eye-spots

JIRI LOCHMAN

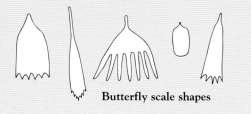
Butterfly scale shapes

Pumping up

After a butterfly emerges from its pupal case it cannot fly, for its wings are limp, folded, creased and damp.

The insect clings to the case, or to another support, while it pumps blood into the wing veins, expanding them. The wings are held apart until they dry, harden and are ready for flight.

An Orchard Swallowtail drying its wings

PETER SLATER

(this species arrived in Australia from North America in about 1870)

butterfly is ready to emerge in its pupal case

PETER MARSACK

The pupal case splits open and the butterfly hauls itself out

PETER MARSACK

The newly emerged butterfly is ready to expand and dry its wings

PETER MARSACK

FACTS

▶ A butterfly's wings lack the spine and hook which couple the fore- and hindwings of moths in flight.

▶ The wings of butterflies and moths may carry "eye-spots", which may scare off predators. Some wings trail "tails", which deflect a hunter's attention from the insect's body.

▶ A butterfly's front pair of feet are often sensitive to odours, especially to the smell of nectar or of a mate.

▶ Some butterfly pupae, like that of the Wanderer Butterfly, hang head downwards. Others, like the Orchard Swallowtail, hang head upwards.

SOME BUTTERFLY EGGS

17

FACTS

▶ The male Regent Skipper is the only butterfly whose wings, like those of moths, are coupled up. A spine on the hindwing links with a hook under the forewing.

▶ The larva of the Moth Butterfly lives inside the nests of the aggressive Green Tree Ant. Protected by a tough, flattened shell, it eats the ant larvae.

▶ The adult Moth Butterfly emerges from its pupa covered with fluffy scales, which protect it from ant attacks. The scales are shed when the butterfly flies.

▶ The rare Bathurst Copper Butterfly is known only from one small area of bush near Bathurst, NSW.

Male Tasmanica Skipper resting with wings held flat

One of the grassdart butterflies rests in typical posture

Two butterfly groups

Two major groups of butterflies are found in Australia.

One group (containing 122 Australian species) includes the skippers and the darts. Their antennae are thickened and hooked towards the ends, and they may rest with the forewings held up and the hindwings flat.

The other group contains four families: the swallowtails (18 species, including the birdwings, triangles, Ulysses and orchard butterflies), the whites (32 species), the browns and fritillaries (85 species) and the blues (140 species).

Kershaw's Brown Butterfly feeding

Ants get the "blues"

The life histories of some butterflies in the "blues" family are interwoven with those of ants. Attempts to rear the caterpillars of these species without ants being present do not succeed.

The caterpillars of some blues live inside ants' nests. Each day, they are led out by the ants to graze on their particular plant food. Others live in the open and are attended by ants as they feed. Sugary fluid produced by the caterpillars is eaten by the ants. A few blues caterpillars prey on ant larvae.

Ictinus Blue Butterflies mating on their offspring's food plant, an acacia

An Ictinus Blue caterpillar attended by meat ants

Butterfly romances

Male butterflies ready to breed appear to recognise females of the same species by sight.

A male may fly up and down above bushes or other vegetation, searching for a mate, or perch on some high point, flying out to intercept passing females.

Once a female appears, the male flutters above her, surrounding her with scent from glands on his wings. If ready to mate, she settles and accepts him.

During mating, which may take several hours, the male passes a packet of sperm to the female. She may store the sperm in her body for some time, until she is ready to lay. Then each of her eggs is fertilised as it passes down the oviduct*.

FACTS

▷ A mating male butterfly of some species becomes unable to move. If the pair is disturbed, the female flies off, carrying him dangling from her abdomen.

▷ The male of some groups of butterflies deposits a substance around the female's reproductive opening after mating with her. This material hardens and forms a plug which prevents other males mating with her.

▷ The compound eye of a butterfly may contain up to 17 000 units. A butterfly is able to see colours, such as ultra-violet, that the eyes of humans cannot perceive.

PETER SLATER

Small Grass Yellow Butterflies mating. The male dangles from the female's abdomen

PETER SLATER

The larvae of the Macleay's Swallowtail will eat the leaves of the introduced* Camphor Laurel

PETER MARSACK

A newly emerged Imperial White Butterfly

BELINDA WRIGHT

Larvae of the Ulysses will eat native Euodia tree leaves

Butterflies in danger

The survival of butterfly species depends on the survival of the plants their caterpillars eat. If these plants disappear, the butterflies dependent on them will disappear also. Rainforest butterflies are particularly vulnerable to destruction of their limited habitat.

An Orchard Swallowtail feeding

STANLEY BREEDEN

19

Night-fliers

The Zodiac Moth flies by day

PETER SLATER

Most Australian moths have a spine or spines on the front edge of the hindwing which fits into a hook on the forewing, coupling them so that the two wings beat together in flight. Only one butterfly, the Regent Skipper, shares this characteristic.

Moths sit with their wings flat and most do not have clubs on the ends of their antennae. Some day-flying moths are brightly coloured and may sometimes be mistaken for butterflies.

PETER SLATER

The male Emperor Gum Moth's feathery antennae help him locate females by scent

Don't eat me!

Caterpillars have soft, juicy bodies, packed with nutritious substances, which are appreciated as food by a wide variety of other animals, so they have developed a number of defences and deceptions to deal with predators.

Some caterpillars depend on camouflage: looper moth caterpillars resemble twigs and stems. Other caterpillars are covered with inedible hairs (though some birds, for example cuckoos, gulp down the meal and bring up the hairs later). Some caterpillars, like the enormous larva of the Hercules Moth, wear formidable-looking (but rubbery) spikes, or flash startling eye-spots. Cup moth larvae wear tufts of spines which can sting an attacker.

Bluff, such as eye-spots, may serve to delay or drive away a predator.

JIRI LOCHMAN

Processionary Caterpillars are ultra-hairy

D. KNOWLES

A noctuid moth caterpillar flashes a rear eye-spot

STANLEY BREEDEN

The spiky final instar of the Hercules Moth caterpillar

WADE HUGHES

A cup moth caterpillar wears tufts of stinging hairs

WADE HUGHES

This looper caterpillar resembles a green stem

Stay-at-home females

The caterpillar of a case moth builds itself a home of tough silk, camouflaged with sticks and leaves. This is dragged behind the owner.

Female case moths do not develop wings. They remain in their mobile homes, while the winged males fly around searching for them.

A case moth caterpillar on the move

Terrible-tasting tigers

The group of tiger moths includes day-fliers whose bright colours advertise that they taste nasty. Some tiger moths produce an evil-tasting froth when they are threatened.

Some of the night-flying tiger moths advertise their identity by broadcasting very high-pitched sounds. Insect-eating bats locate prey by sending out such ultrasound*, so they are able to pick up the moth's signal easily. Once a bat has bitten one of these moths and found out it is inedible, it associates the warning with the distasteful experience and leaves a broadcasting moth alone.

A tiger moth may produce nasty chemical froth

The Hercules Moth is Australia's largest moth

This plume moth has divided, feathery wings

Hawk moths are strong fliers, and can hover in front of flowers to suck out nectar

A male whistling moth makes high-pitched sounds which may be part of courtship

FACTS

▶ Moths can detect light at a distance. One species can see the radiation from a 15-watt ultraviolet lamp at a distance of 250 m.

▶ A geometrid moth has ears at the base of the abdomen.

▶ The Bogong Moth breeds in southeastern Australia's inland in winter. Adults migrate each year to spend summer in the mountains of southeastern NSW. Aboriginal tribes used to gather to feast on these moths.

▶ Australia's largest moth, the Hercules Moth (wingspan up to 27 cm) is one of the biggest moths in the world. Its caterpillar may be 100 mm long.

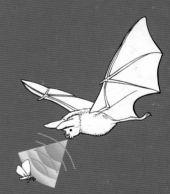

This bat is receiving echoes from its own ultrasound bouncing off the moth, as well as receiving ultrasound given out by the moth. Once a hungry bat has sampled a broadcasting, nasty-tasting moth, it should leave other broadcasting moths alone.

21

FACTS

▶ The order Diptera (two-wings) includes flies, mosquitoes, midges, sand flies, March flies, robber flies, fruit flies, bee flies and others.

▶ Fly larvae, or maggots, have no true legs, and tiny heads. Most live in damp places and many swim in their food.

▶ Flies eat solid food by first dissolving it in saliva, then sucking up the liquid.

▶ Robber flies are large, strong-legged insects which capture other insects in flight, then hold them while sucking out their juices.

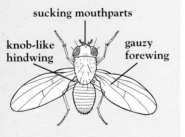

sucking mouthparts
knob-like hindwing · gauzy forewing

A TYPICAL FLY

Wings of gauze

The insects on these two pages all have transparent wings with obvious veins. They are placed in three unrelated groups of insects.

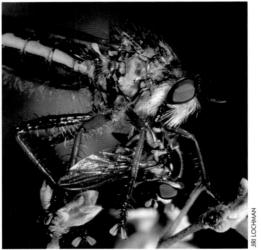
A robber fly eating a hover-fly

Yellow-headed Bristle Fly

Two wings, two balancers

Flies, midges and mosquitoes are "two-winged" insects, whose hindwings are reduced to small, club-shaped knobs, used for balancing, and for judging speed and the position of the owner's body.

The mouthparts are adapted for sucking, and sometimes for piercing. Often saliva is introduced into the food, which is then sucked up. Some insects in this group have lifestyles that affect humans and domestic animals.

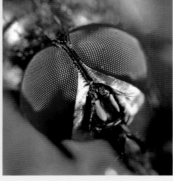

How to sex Bush Flies

The female Bush Fly (far left) has its eyes set wide apart. The male (left) has eyes which nearly touch on the top of its head.

Growing up in a trap

Pitcher-plants trap insects, then digest the bodies. The maggot of the wingless fly *Badesis ambulans* lives unharmed in the liquid contained in the Albany Pitcher-plant. It feeds on the plant's victims, becomes a pupa, then emerges as a nectar-eating adult.

Adult, wingless *Badesis ambulans* on tea-tree blossom

Albany Pitcher-plant

A multitude of lifestyles

This bee fly will transport pollen to the next flower it visits

JIRI LOCHMAN

There are many different and fascinating flies, with a wide variety of lifestyles.
Bee flies look like wasps or bees but have no sting. Hover flies dart amongst flowers and hover over them while feeding. Fruit flies feed inside ripening fruit and may be serious agricultural pests. Vinegar flies live in decaying fruit, blowflies eat carrion or infest wounds, stable flies suck blood from large animals. There are even blood-sucking flies which live only on the skins of birds.

Only females suck blood

D. KNOWLES

The world's largest mosquito is found in Queensland. The female of this species does not suck blood

Australia has over 200 species of mosquito. The males live on plant juices, but most females suck blood, necessary for the development of their eggs, from other animals. In the process, they may transmit diseases such as malaria, dengue fever and Ross River virus to humans, heartworm to dogs, and myxomatosis to rabbits (see also p. 46).

(see also p. 46)

ANT-LIONS AND LACEWINGS

JIRI LOCHMAN

Ant-lion larva hides at the bottom of a sandpit trap

Ant-lions and lacewings form the order Neuroptera ("nerve-wings"). The adults have gauzy wings, whose many veins give them a lacy appearance. The larvae are predators, sucking the juices of insect prey. Ant-lion larvae ambush prey, hiding in pit traps they have dug in sand.

PETER SLATER

An adult Golden-eyed Lacewing

SCORPION FLIES

Scorpion flies are long-headed, long-legged insects with two pairs of membranous wings. The male's long abdomen is sometimes curled over like that of a scorpion. Although called "flies", they are placed in an order of their own, the order Mecoptera, or "long-wings".

Scorpion fly larvae eat dead insects and plants, and adults feed on insects, caught with their grappling hindlegs. A courting male catches an insect and gives it to a female. Like the female shown underneath the male at right, she eats the male's gift while mating with him.

D. KNOWLES

Mating scorpion flies

Activity unlimited

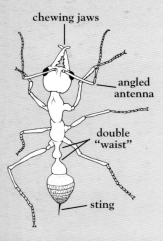

A WORKER ANT

- chewing jaws
- angled antenna
- double "waist"
- sting

Ants have a second "waist" between the second and third segments of the abdomen. Fertile adults have two pairs of membranous wings. Ant larvae are maggot-like and legless.

A nest of ants contains several castes of individuals.

Queens are fertile females which shed their wings after mating, then lay eggs. A nest may contain more than one queen.

Males are winged and fertile. Their only role is to mate with the queens.

Workers are wingless, infertile* females. **Soldiers** are aggressive, strong-jawed workers.

Home, crowded home

Ants usually live in colonies, in nests which may be sited in crevices in trees, rocks or buildings or excavated underground. Each caste has its own job within the nest. Queens and males are breeders. Workers feed the colony and take care of larvae and pupae. Soldiers defend the colony.

An ant shifting a pebble

Ants tending pupae

Ants attacking a grasshopper

Green Tree Ants pull leaves together to make a nest

This katydid nymph mimics a Green Tree Ant

Buried treasure

Some species of ants have special workers called repletes. These are fed by the other workers and store nectar in their abdomens. They give up this rich nourishment on request. Honey Pot Ants, dug from their nests, are a traditional Aboriginal source of sweetness.

Honey Pot Ants' abdomens are storage containers
STANLEY BREEDEN

World's most primitive

Nothomyrmecia macrops, the world's most primitive ant, was discovered in the form of two specimens in Victoria's National Museum insect collection in 1934. The ants had been collected in 1932, between Balladonia and Mt Ragged, Western Australia. In spite of several searches, this large ant was not reported again until 1977, when CSIRO scientists discovered it on the Eyre Peninsula, South Australia.

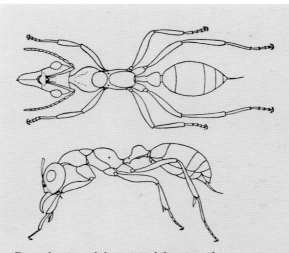
Reproduction of the original drawing of *Nothomyrmecia macrops* (live insect is 1.3 cm long)

A Bull Ant retrieving a dead scarab beetle
JIRI LOCHMAN

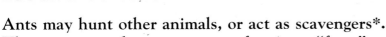
The Thorny Devil lizard specialises in eating small ants
JIRI LOCHMAN

Eat and be eaten

Ants may hunt other animals, or act as scavengers*. They may eat plants, nectar or fungi, or "farm" caterpillars, scale insects or aphids for the sweet liquids they produce.

Australian animals which specialise in eating ants include the Short-beaked Echidna, the Thorny Devil, other lizards, some frogs and burrowing blind snakes.

D. KNOWLES

These ants from the Great Sandy Desert feed at night

Gatherers of sweetness

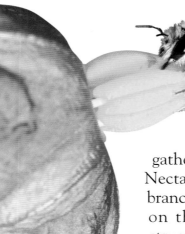

A solitary burrowing bee

The second segment of the abdomen of a bee or a wasp is elongated to form a "waist" (very marked in some wasps). The lower lips of bees form a "tongue", with which they obtain nectar.

Most bees are solitary*, some nest in social* groups, and others live in large hives. They gather nectar and pollen to eat, and to feed their larvae. Nectar is collected with the tongue, while pollen sticks to branched hairs on the underside of the bee's abdomen and on the legs. Pollen may be carried in a basket-like structure on the hindleg, or in a crop inside the body.

A female solitary burrowing bee digging her nest burrow

A social burrowing bee gathering nectar

A WORKER BEE

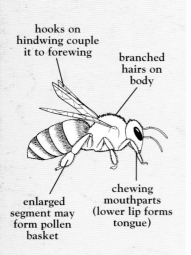

hooks on hindwing couple it to forewing

branched hairs on body

enlarged segment may form pollen basket

chewing mouthparts (lower lip forms tongue)

Solitary bees

The group of burrowing solitary bees, which includes the carpenter and mortar bees, contains Australia's largest bees.

The carpenter bees are very hairy and often wear metallic colours. They make their nests in burrows excavated in wood or in the stems of plants.

Mortar bees, like Dawson's Burrowing Bee at right, wear bands of colour. They usually nest in burrows in the soil, but may rake out mortar from between bricks to make holes for their nests.

A Dawson's Burrowing Bee peers from its nest burrow

A social burrowing bee gathering pollen

A Red-faced Mastic Bee on a grevillea flower

Honey in the hive

The introduced Honey Bee sets up feral* hives in suitable hollows in the Australian bush.

Each hive contains honeycombs made up of thousands of six-sided wax cells. Each cell contains honey, which the worker bees produce from nectar.

When a worker finds a good source of nectar and pollen, it returns to the hive and dances in a figure-eight pattern. Other workers observe the dance, then fly to the location of the food source.

Larvae which will grow up to be infertile workers are fed on bee-bread, made of honey and pollen. Larvae which will be fertile queens are fed on more nutritious royal jelly. A young queen mates with a drone, a fertile male, then begins to lay eggs. If a hive becomes over-crowded, an older queen may lead a swarm to found a new hive.

Sugarbag!

The small, black, native honey bees do not sting. They may be attracted by human secretions and are sometimes called "sweat bees".

Their other name, "sugarbag bees", is due to the fact that their honey is prized by the Aboriginal people. The hives are chopped out of tree hollows, or combs and honey are scooped from crevices in rocks.

Native honey bees extending their hive's entrance

Note hairs on eyes of this introduced Honey Bee

Feral Honey Bees on honeycombs in a cave

FACTS

▶ A bee's fore- and hindwings are held together by a row of hooks.

▶ The introduced Honey Bee can be told from most native species by the fact that it has hairs growing from its eyes.

▶ A Honey Bee may beat its wings 200 times per second when in flight.

▶ When a worker Honey Bee stings, its sting is torn away and remains in the victim. The mutilated bee dies.

▶ Cuckoo bees lay their eggs in the nests of other bees. The parasite's larvae steal the host's stored food.

▶ Leafcutting bees are solitary bees which cut semi-circular pieces from the edges of leaves, then use them to make nests in holes in wood or in the ground.

Leaf damaged by leaf-cutting bees

27

DID YOU KNOW?

FACTS

▶ The breeding habits of the monsters in the *Alien* series of films were probably inspired by the way in which many wasps lay their eggs in living hosts.

▶ Some hunter wasps hide their prey, and the eggs laid on it, in burrows. After the burrow is filled, one of these wasps may use a stone held in her jaws to hammer the soil firmly into place. She thus joins the ranks of tool-using animals.

A wasp's tool-using jaws

▶ A hunter wasp locates prey by vision or scent and immobilises it by stinging it once or several times. Each group of wasps has its own method of carrying prey. Some carry it in the jaws, some with the middle legs, some with the hindlegs, or even impaled on the sting.

Hunters and storers

Many wasps parasitise* and prey upon other insects and spiders. They sting and paralyse them, then lay eggs on them. These eggs will hatch into larvae, which will eat their hosts. (Adult wasps eat fluids, such as nectar.)

Ichneumon wasps use their long ovipositors to lay eggs in, or on, the body of a host such as a caterpillar or a grasshopper. Flower wasps parasitise the larvae of beetles. Hunter wasps stock their nests with paralysed spiders or insects and lay eggs upon them. After the larvae hatch, they devour these living stores. Paper nest wasps are social and build nests of six-sided cells. They chew up caterpillar flesh for their larvae.

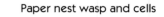

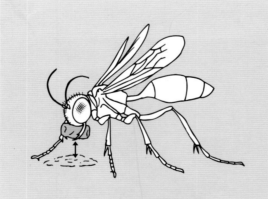

A wasp tamping soil into place with a stone.

A spider-hunting wasp dragging a spider to her nest

Paper nest wasp and cells

Paper nest wasps on their nest in rainforest

Spider-hunters

A spider-hunting wasp may sting, and paralyse, a spider many times her own size. The spider is dragged to a nest burrow, stored inside and an egg laid on it. When the wasp larva hatches, it eats the immobilised spider before pupating. The wasp recognises the position of her burrow by memorising landmarks. If the landmarks are changed, she may "lose" the burrow.

28

Mud-dauber wasps mating on water

A female mud-dauber wasp with her caterpillar victim

A mud-dauber carrying a paralysed caterpillar to her nest, using jaws and six legs to support the burden

A mud-dauber laying her egg inside a mud cell

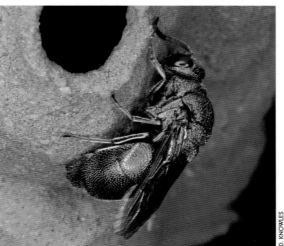
A cuckoo wasp investigating a mud-dauber's nest

FACTS

▶ The European wasp now lives in south-eastern Australia. The worker is 12–15 mm long, with a black and yellow banded body. A nest may contain over 100 000 workers. The sting is painful to humans and a wasp may sting several times.

▶ Cuckoo wasps lay their own eggs in the nests of hunter wasps. Their larvae eat the prey and the hunter wasps' larvae as well.

▶ When attacked by the owner of a nest, a cuckoo wasp curls up into a ball. The hunter wasp cannot sting it through its armour-like exoskeleton.

▶ Mud-dauber wasps may remain near their nests, apparently "guarding" them, for some time after laying in them and sealing them.

A sleeping wasp secures itself by clinging to a twig with its jaws

FACTS

▸ There are around 750 species of flower wasps in Australia.

▸ Gall wasps lay their eggs into the young stems of trees. As the larva develops, the plant tissue around it forms a woody gall.

▸ The citrus gall wasp once bred in native trees related to citrus. It now affects oranges, lemons and other cultivated citrus.

▸ The Sirex Wasp was accidentally introduced into Australia in the 1940s and now is a pest in Vic. and Tas. pine forests.

▸ The female Sirex Wasp bores into the sapwood of a tree and deposits eggs and the spores of a fungus. The fungus is necessary for development of the larvae, but harms the tree.

▸ Efforts to control the Sirex Wasp have included the introduction from overseas of two ichneumon wasps which parasitise the Sirex.

A male flower wasp feeding on scale insect fluids

A male flower wasp carrying a feeding female

Not an ant but a wasp

A female velvet ant is covered with hairs and has no wings. It lays eggs on the larvae of bees and other wasps.

Velvet ants are wingless females of a family of wasps

Dependent females

The lives of flower wasps are entwined with the life histories of Australia's flowering plants.

The adult wasps feed on nectar. In the process, they become dusted with pollen, which they transport to other flowers, fertilising them.

The female flower wasp has no wings and her legs are specialised* for digging into soil to locate the beetle larvae on which she will lay her eggs. The mating organs on the tip of her abdomen become attached to those of a male, who carries her to food and may feed her mouth-to-mouth. Flower wasps feed on nectar, or on the liquid produced by scale insects or lerps (insects which suck eucalyptus sap).

A male flower wasp carrying and feeding a female

A male flower wasp carrying pollen capsules

30

This slipper orchid sends out a scent resembling the odour of a female ichneumon wasp, which lures male wasps. The orchid is shaped so that when the wasp "mates" with it pollen is deposited on the insect. The wasp then flies to another orchid and "mates" with it, in the process depositing the pollen from the first flower.

A male ichneumon wasp carries a pollen packet on its abdomen after "mating" with a slipper orchid

An adult sawfly has no "waist" and does not sting

Sawfly larvae are commonly known as "spitfires"

FACTS

▶ The female sawfly slits a leaf with the saw-like tip of her ovipositor and lays an egg inside. Sawfly larvae resemble tough-skinned, spiky-haired caterpillars. They feed on leaves, and some may "spit" out nasty liquids.

Wings in sheaths

Head and forelegs of a burrowing ground beetle

The membranous hindwings of beetles and weevils fold away neatly under the tough, hard, rigid forewings. These armoured forewings, known as elytra*, meet without overlap and protect the abdomen. An adult beetle or weevil has chewing mouthparts. The larvae of these insects have hard heads, chewing mouthparts and, usually, legs.

A variety of lifestyles

Beetles live in almost every available land and freshwater habitat and obtain food in many different ways.

Some, such as tiger beetles, are predators on insects and other small creatures. Some feed on nectar or plant liquids. Some live in the nests of other animals, such as termites, produce substances which are eaten by their hosts and in turn feed on the hosts, or on food stored in the nest. Some beetle larvae need the help of fungi to make their plant food source digestible and may transport the spores of the fungi when they change food sources.

Beetles may eat or damage stored human food or other possessions.

As a jewel beetle takes off, the elytra are held rigid while the membranous hindwings vibrate

This predatory tiger beetle, which lives on salt lakes, is eating a fly

The powerful jaws of a tree-living tiger beetle

A male stag beetle with pincer jaws

The larva of this longicorn bores into Tuart trees

The larva of a rainforest stag beetle

The pupa of a stag beetle shows massive mandibles*

This adult male stag beetle has colourful elytra

Sneaky may win a prize

Male stag beetles have enlarged jaws, which they may use to battle for females. However, while two male beetles are locked in combat, a third male, which may have only small weapons, may sneak in and mate with the female.

Underwater hunters

Diving beetles are found in most fresh water. They row with their fringed hind legs and breathe by poking the tip of the abdomen above the surface, sucking in air which is stored under the elytra. An adult diving beetle may be four centimetres long and capable of catching small fish.

A diving beetle hunting for aquatic prey

FACTS

▶ The oldest beetle-like fossils date to about 280 million years ago. True beetles appeared about 240 million years ago.

▶ The world's largest beetle, 20 cm long, lives in the Amazon Basin of South America. The body of Wallace's Longicorn, from Cape York, Qld, is 8 cm long and its antennae 12 cm.

▶ To defend themselves, some beetles produce noxious substances, such as hydrogen cyanide. The bombardier beetles keep chemicals stored in their bodies, then combine them when needed. The resulting mixture shoots out with a puff of smoke and an explosive noise.

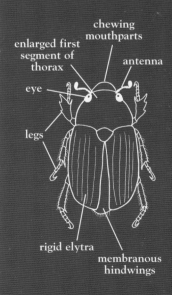
chewing
mouthparts
enlarged first
segment of
thorax
antenna
eye
legs
rigid elytra
membranous
hindwings

A TYPICAL BEETLE

FACTS

▶ Beetles have been introduced as biological* controls on pest plants such as Lantana, Prickly Pear, Giant Sensitive Plant and Ragwort.

▶ Scarab beetles include dung beetles. Their larvae have a typical "C" shape and live on rotting vegetation, in soil and in manure.

▶ Dung beetles feed on animal droppings and bury pellets of this substance as food for their larvae.

▶ Dung beetles have been introduced from South Africa and the Mediterranean region to control cattle dung and thus bush flies. Native dung beetles cope best with the pelleted droppings of native mammals.

Ladybirds

Australia has around 300 species of ladybirds. They are circular, rounded beetles whose legs and antennae are hidden under their bodies. As both larvae and adults, most species eat other insects, including agricultural pests such as aphids, scale insects and mites.

A Eucalyptus Leaf Beetle
JIRI LOCHMAN

A congregation of ladybirds
JIRI LOCHMAN

A scarab beetle larva in a typical curled "C" posture
WADE HUGHES

A rainforest scarab beetle
D. KNOWLES

Weevil-doers

Weevils are dull-coloured beetles with very hard bodies. Their long snouts have mouthparts at their ends. Weevil larvae live in wood or plant tissues, and introduced weevils are important pests, whose larvae eat stored human food, especially grain.

Longicorn beetle about to take wing
STANLEY BREEDEN

Feel no weevil

In at least 50 species of weevils, females can reproduce without mating with males. This "virgin birth" produces only female offspring. Mating with a male is necessary to produce males as well as females.

Mating weevils each contribute to their offspring
JIRI LOCHMAN

A pair of Roe's Jewel Beetles mating. Jewel beetles are often colourful and appear metallic

A jewel beetle feeding on Desert Starflower

Round the bend

When mating, a male beetle may use special leg spines to grip the female's rigid, curved back. At the end of his abdomen, he has a penis* which allows him to reach around and under the female's body to deliver his sperm. For better access, the penis may be curved.

A rainforest jewel beetle from North Queensland

Male jewel beetles on a beer bottle which satisfies their visual requirements for a female

35

Aerial predators

A damselfly is built for aerial agility

STANLEY BREEDEN

Dragonflies and damselflies are strong-flying, often brightly coloured predators.

They have huge compound eyes, three simple eyes and tiny, pointed antennae. The mouthparts have toothed jaws adapted for biting and the legs end in clawed segments suited to grabbing and holding prey while it is killed and eaten.

Dragonflies and damselflies lay their eggs in fresh water. The larvae feed on aquatic animals, then finally leave the water and emerge as winged adults.

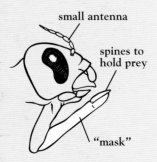

small antenna

spines to hold prey

"mask"

A side view of a dragonfly nymph's head, showing the "mask" which shoots out to catch victims

A dragonfly's huge eyes and powerful thorax

PETER MARSACK

Terror in a mask

A dragonfly larva catches small water creatures by shooting out a long lower lip, which is normally folded below the head. The victim is impaled on hooks and spines at the tip of the "mask", which is then folded back so the prey can be eaten. The mask is activated by a pumping action of the larva's abdomen (which also powers the "jet" movement of the larva and sends water over the gills).

A dew-sprinkled dragonfly roosts with wings flat

PETER MARSACK

Dragonflies

Dragonflies are stouter-bodied and stronger-flying than damselflies.

A dragonfly's forewings are differently shaped and veined from the hindwings, and are held flat or bowed downwards when the insect is at rest. A dragonfly larva has internal gills, concealed in its rectum*.

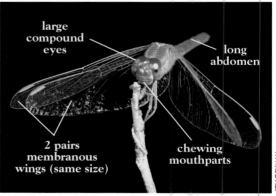

large compound eyes

long abdomen

2 pairs membranous wings (same size)

chewing mouthparts

JIRI LOCHMAN

Dragonfly roosting with wings held flat and bowed

Damselflies

Damselflies are more slender-bodied than dragonflies. Their fore- and hindwings are similar in shape and veining and are held closed along the body when the insect rests. A damselfly larva has exposed gills extending like three fine leaves at the end of the body.

A damselfly larva, with head at right and exposed gills at top left

WADE HUGHES

Sperm wars

A male dragonfly or damselfly will scoop another male's sperm out of a female before mating with her. To prevent the same thing happening to his sperm, he flies linked to her while she lays the eggs he has fertilised.

JIRI LOCHMAN

A newly emerged dragonfly clings to its pupal case

PETER MARSACK

A dew-covered female (above) and male damselfly (below) roosting, wings folded on bodies

Mating dragonflies adopt a "wheel" position, in which the male holds the female's neck with the end of his abdomen. The female bends the tip of her abdomen forward to pick up sperm the male has previously deposited on the second segment of his abdomen.

PETER MARSACK

Male (left) and female dragonflies mating

FACTS

▶ Some dragonflies perch much of the time, while others spend most time cruising on the wing. Damselflies are perchers.

▶ A male dragonfly or damselfly will establish a territory* and defend it against other males. He grasps a female by the neck and they mate in wheel position (see below). She lays her eggs in water, sometimes still in tandem with the male.

Prophets that prey

Praying mantids are predators, which seize other insects or invertebrates with forelegs armed with one or two rows of sharp spines. The two compound eyes are very large, there are three simple* eyes and the head is very mobile. The first segment of the thorax is elongated. The forewings are hard and protect the membranous hindwings. Some female mantids may be wingless.

A hunting mantid stalks its prey or waits in ambush, then shoots out its forelegs to seize the prey. Most are brown or green and well camouflaged in vegetation. Some mantids which live in grasses may change colour from green to brown with the season.

A praying mantid cleaning its spined foreleg

A praying mantid eating a grasshopper

Eggs in foam

A female praying mantid lays up to several hundred eggs, surrounded by a frothy liquid which hardens to form a case. This egg case may be found on plants, or under logs or stones.

A female mantid laying eggs surrounded by foam

This praying mantid matches the colour of dead leaves

PHASMIDS
Deceivers

Australia's Giant Phasmid may grow to 25 cm in length. It is a harmless plant-eater

Phasmids (stick or leaf insects) have very slender, elongated or flattened bodies, and most resemble sticks, stems or leaves. This protective camouflage is very successful while the insect remains still; most species move around and feed at night.

Phasmid nymphs resemble wingless adults; the wings increase in size with each moult. When the insect is adult, the forewings only partly cover the hindwings. Females may be flightless. Most phasmid females drop their shiny, seed-like eggs to the ground, and females of some species may lay fertile eggs without having mated with males.

JIRI LOCHMAN

Phasmid nymph

A Giant Phasmid eating an acacia flower

A rainforest phasmid from North Queensland

FACTS

▶ The category Phasmodea which is applied to phasmids means "like a ghost", referring to their ability to blend with their background.

▶ There are around 150 Australian species of phasmids. Three are leaf insects, the remainder stick insects.

▶ In self-defence, a phasmid may suddenly open bright wings, hiss, or kick with spiny hindlegs. Some species freeze, some regurgitate food, some spray an irritating chemical.

▶ The eggs of some phasmids have a white fatty knob at one end. Ants take the eggs underground, then eat the knobs. The eggs, protected from fire and parasites, eventually hatch and the young phasmids dig to the surface.

Suckers

Bugs, cicadas and the other Hemiptera exist in many forms and colours. All suck up their food and have mouthparts which are fused into a long, sharply pointed beak.

A bug-spotter may divide Hemiptera into three recognisable groups: the true bugs, the hoppers (which includes cicadas) and the scale insects, aphids and lerps.

A true bug's forewings are hard at the bases and membranous at the tips. They sit flat, hiding the membranous hindwings. The head and beak can flex* forwards.

A hopper's forewings are all the same texture and are held tented over the body. The head and beak point down and back.

Aphids, scale insects, mealy bugs and lerps usually have soft bodies and no wings, or only forewings. Their heads and beaks point down and back. Often they cover themselves with wax or froth, which prevents their soft bodies drying out.

PETER MARSACK

A female bug guarding her eggs

D. KNOWLES

A jewel bug

JIRI LOCHMAN

An assassin bug, showing its stabbing and sucking beak

Assassination by stabbing

Most true bugs feed on plant sap, but the assassin bugs hunt insects.

The bug leaps from ambush onto its prey, grabs it with its front legs, then plunges its beak into the victim. The bug then injects saliva, so the insect's body contents are digested before they are sucked up through the beak.

The pinhead-sized eggs of a "true bug"
PETER MARSACK

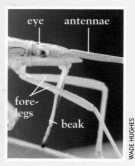

Some bugs walk on water

Water striders glide across the surface film of fresh water. Backswimmers swim upside down. Water scorpions live under water, in mud or debris. Water-boatmen trap air under their wings to allow them to feed under water. Giant water bugs swim using strong, hairy hindlegs: they feed on small water creatures.

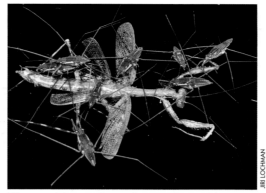

Water striders eating a drowned mantid

A leaf-hopper attended by an ant

A Long-winged Hopper

Double drummers

Cicadas are stout-bodied insects with two pairs of membranous wings. A cicada nymph may spend years underground, feeding on root sap. Finally it emerges, climbs a tree or other vertical object, and emerges from its larval skin as a winged adult.

A male cicada makes a distinctive call by vibrating drum-like membranes situated on either side of his abdomen. The sound, amplified* by air sacs in the abdomen, may reach 100 decibels in loudness. A female cicada lays her eggs in slits cut into tree bark. The newly hatched nymphs fall to the ground and dig in with their large front legs.

Self-sufficient females

Many aphid species in Australia were introduced to the country accidentally. Some female aphids give birth to only females, which produce other females during summer. As winter approaches, males are produced as well; these fertilise females whose eggs hatch the following springtime.

Aphids (see p. 47), scale insects, mealy bugs, gall insects, lerps, leaf-hoppers and spittle bugs all feed on plants. They suck sap from leaves and stems, and some are pests which damage garden and commercial crop plants.

A cicada freshly emerged from its larval skin

(see p. 47)

FACTS

▶ Backswimmers have keel-shaped backs. Grooves down the abdomen hold hairs which trap air to use when submerged.

▶ A Giant Water Bug may fly into a house at night, attracted by the light. If picked up, it may pretend to be dead, but can stab a human hand with its beak.

Unicorn Lantern-fly

▶ Lantern-flies are tropical leafhoppers. Some species have a long horn pointing forward from the head.

▶ A cicada's ears are on either side of its abdomen.

▶ Cicadas take a long time to develop into adults because of the poor quality of their watery sap food. A species of North American cicada may spend 17 years underground.

Leapers

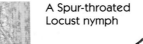

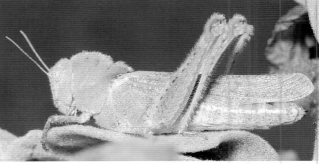

A Spur-throated Locust nymph

A short-horned grasshopper on its food plant

Grasshoppers and crickets have large hindlegs, usually used for jumping. The first segment of the thorax is well developed, and narrow, tough forewings protect the larger, wider, membranous hindwings. These insects have chewing mouthparts. In many species, to attract females, the males produce loud calls by rubbing parts of the legs, wings and/or abdomen on each other.

Shorthorns

Short-horned, or true, grasshoppers have antennae less than 30 segments long (usually less than half the insect's body-length) and live on plants near the ground, often in grasses. They feed during the day, and the males make simple clicks and chirps.

Locusts are grasshoppers which occur in swarms and cause great damage to crops and pastures. A single locust eats its own weight in plant food every day. A locust nymph can jump ten times its own length and travel ten metres in a minute.

chewing mouthparts

antennae

large eye

large, muscular hindlegs used for leaping

tough, narrow forewings cover wide, membranous hindwings

An adult Spur-throated Locust

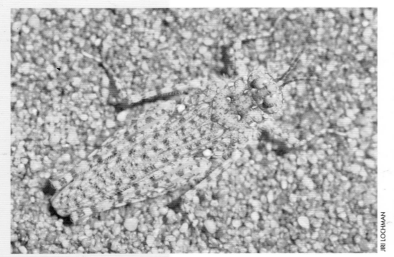

This sand-dune grasshopper blends into the background

A long-headed grasshopper nymph is camouflaged in green grass

The mole cricket burrows underground

A female king cricket laying eggs through her ovipositor

Crickets and katydids

Crickets have very long antennae (usually more than 30 segments in length). Their ears are on their front legs. Most crickets are active at night, revealing their presence by sometimes long and complex songs. A female cricket has a particularly long ovipositor, which projects from the end of her abdomen.

One group of crickets is commonly known as "katydids". They often live in foliage and are often green in colour.

The Cooloola Monster

A strange, humpbacked, almost blind insect with shovel-like legs and only traces of wings was first discovered at Cooloola, Queensland, in 1977. It was sent to a world-wide expert on the order Orthoptera, who thought this odd creature was a man-made hoax.

The "Cooloola Monster" is a cricket which, with three related species, lives in the sandy, moist soils of Queensland's coasts, feeding on other burrowers.

A katydid wears camouflage colours

FACTS

▶ King crickets are predators with powerful jaws, which live in Australia's east-coast forests. They are related to the famous wetas of New Zealand.

▶ Mole crickets, which have powerful digging forelegs, live in burrows. Their loud songs are amplified by the shapes of their burrow entrances.

▶ The Frog-eating Cricket of southeastern Qld pulls one of a small tree-frog's hindlegs slowly back. With its leg pinned back, the frog cannot jump away, and the cricket eats first the leg then the frog's body.

▶ Australia has 42 species of tiny wingless crickets which live inside ant nests.

The head, antennae and spiny limbs of a bush cricket

The massive jaws of a male king cricket

43

Recyclers

Termites are pale-bodied insects with chewing mouthparts and antennae which look like strings of beads. Each species of termite includes a number of different castes.

Termites live in colonies, in nests of earth and digestive wastes they build in, or on, wood or the ground. They eat wood and other plant matter, digesting the cellulose* it contains with the aid of micro-organisms living in their digestive tracts.

This enormous mound was built by tiny, blind termite workers

Termite society

Within a termite colony there are several castes.

Winged, fertile **alates*** fly from the nest on humid nights. A pair of alates shed their wings, mate, then begin a new nest. They then become the fertile **"queen"** and **"king"** which produce all the castes.

The sterile*, blind **workers** build and maintain the nest, feed other castes and look after the queen.

The sterile, blind, strongly-built **soldiers** protect the nest.

Immature **nymphs** develop into workers, soldiers, or winged, fertile alates, which begin the cycle again.

Large-jawed termite soldiers ready for defence

Blind termite workers in action in a piece of wood

Alates ready to shed their wings and reproduce

Runways protect termites from exposure to light

ANT OR "WHITE ANT"?

Termites are sometimes wrongly called "white ants". However, termite and ant workers can be told apart quite easily as shown below.

TERMITE

no eyes
straight antennae
no defined "waist"
paler, softer body

ANT

compound eyes
angled antennae
two "waists"
darker, harder body

These pointy-nosed soldier termites can shoot an unpleasant fluid from their snouts

THE USEFUL TERMITE

A Forest Kingfisher digs a nest in a tree termite mound

Many reptiles, like this Frilled Lizard, eat termites

The Numbat eats termites scratched from their runways or from wood weakened by their activities

The Short-beaked Echidna claws open mounds

DID YOU KNOW?

FACTS
INSECTS WHICH CAN CARRY DISEASES, OR PARASITES, OF HUMANS

▶ **mosquito** (malaria parasite, Ross River virus, Murray Valley encephalitis)

rat flea (bubonic plague, typhus, tapeworms)

dog flea (tapeworms)

buffalo gnat, sand fly and horse fly (parasitic roundworms)

louse (*Rickettsia*, typhus)

house fly (typhoid, diarrhoea, dysentery)

Them and us

Around 1000 species of insects directly interact with human lives. In Australia, some of the most important "pests" were introduced from overseas.

Insect pests eat around one-third of all agricultural produce in the field, then consume a further one-quarter in storage. Insects may carry diseases or parasites which attack humans or domesticated animals. Insects also destroy trees, and timber in buildings and other constructions.

However, those 1000 species of insects which humans regard as "harmful" form only a fraction of the 1 000 000 so far named by science.

Insects are vital to the world as we know it. Plant-eating insects are the basis of most of the animal food-chains on dry land, being eaten by larger animals, which in turn are eaten by other creatures. Insects pollinate many sorts of flowers. They break down vegetation, dead and living.

Quite apart from their "useful" or "harmful" qualities (and from its own point of view an insect which multiplies to numbers which harm human interests is being very successful) insects are fascinating. For example, the cockroach is so well-adapted to its lifestyle that it has not updated its form or functioning to any great extent in the past 300 million years.

The introduced Rice Weevil lays eggs in stored grain. Each larva eats out a grain before pupating in the husk

The introduced Black Carpet Beetle larva devours both wool and hides

The introduced silverfish eats wallpaper, book covers and fabrics

The introduced Indian House Cricket is a noisy house-guest

The introduced American Cockroach fouls food

Care for a caterpillar snack?

Many insects are eaten by humans in various parts of the world. Creatures such as water bugs, locusts, cicadas and bee larvae are favoured items of diet in South-East Asia and Africa. In Australia, the Bogong Moth, hawkmoth caterpillars, termites and "witchetty grubs" (the larvae of longicorn beetles and cossid moths) were traditional Aboriginal foods. Bogong Moths contain 27 per cent protein and 20 per cent fat: many other insects are just as nutritious.

Fast-breeding aphids on a citrus tree

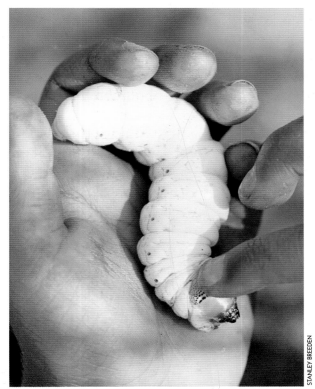

This "witchetty grub" is the larva of a moth

Insects v. pesticides

Plants may produce poisons which make them unpalatable* or toxic* to insects. Humans use these natural pesticides, such as nicotine and pyrethrum, to kill insects.

Manufactured pesticides can be deadly to insects, but may also poison other animals, including humans. The pest insect may in time acquire resistance to the chemical and survive its use, while other animals are still affected.

Unlike some introduced relatives, these insects do not affect humans

The elegant Australian Painted Earwig is no threat to gardens

An Australian bush cockroach carrying its egg case on its abdomen

▶ Bot Fly larvae develop in the guts of horses. In order to control these pests (and other parasites such as roundworms), horse owners dose their animals with chemical "wormers". The chemicals remaining in the horse's manure can kill dung beetles.

▶ Prickly pear cactus was introduced to Australia in the early 1800s to feed the dye-producing Cochineal Insect. By 1925, prickly pear had spread over 25 million hectares of agricultural land.

▶ In 1925, the *Cactoblastis* moth was introduced from Argentina. The moth caterpillars ate the prickly pear and saved thousands of farmers from ruin. At Boonarga, Qld, there stands a Memorial Hall dedicated to the *Cactoblastis* moth.

▶ The fern *Salvinia* and Water Hyacinth, introduced pest weeds on fresh water, are controlled with the help of two species of South American weevil.

Pestilent flies

In order to eat solid food, House Flies vomit up digestive juices, which turn the food into liquid which can be sucked up. A House Fly may carry millions of bacteria* in its gut, or in its mouthparts, or on its feet. Some fly species, such as the winged March Fly and Buffalo Fly, and the wingless Sheep Ked and Wallaby Fly, suck blood from animals.

The larvae, or maggots, of many sorts of flies develop in manure, in dead animals or in rotting vegetable matter. Introduced dung beetles, whose larvae feed on manure, have proved successful biological controls on Bush Flies and House Flies in some parts of Australia.

Introduced dung beetle

A female March Fly sucking up human blood

A blowfly lays eggs in manure or decaying flesh

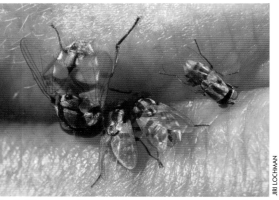
Bush Flies are attracted to moisture on human lips

A House Fly can transmit disease in its saliva

Biological controls

Biological controls work best where the predator destroys only the pest species, nearly wipes it out, then remains scarce itself. This means a small number of predators continues to control a small number of pests without either becoming common.

Before introducing a biological control from overseas, scientists must conduct many tests to make sure the control does not "run wild". The 1930s introduction of the Cane Toad to eat insect pests of sugar cane led to the toad itself becoming a pest species, and a harmful influence on many native Australian animals.

A female mosquito (not a malaria-carrying species) with a gut full of human blood

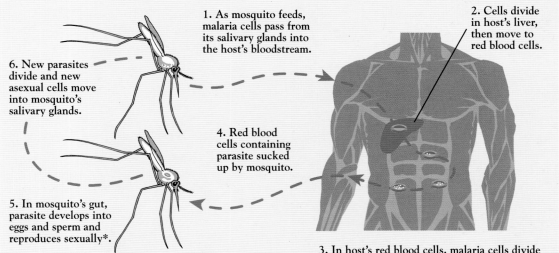

1. As mosquito feeds, malaria cells pass from its salivary glands into the host's bloodstream.

2. Cells divide in host's liver, then move to red blood cells.

6. New parasites divide and new asexual cells move into mosquito's salivary glands.

4. Red blood cells containing parasite sucked up by mosquito.

5. In mosquito's gut, parasite develops into eggs and sperm and reproduces sexually*.

3. In host's red blood cells, malaria cells divide asexually* every 48 or 72 hours, releasing toxins which cause cycles of fever and chills.

LIFE CYCLE OF THE MALARIA PARASITE

The introduced Green Vegetable Bug laying eggs

A tree killed by longicorn beetle larvae

FACTS
ABOUT MOSQUITOES AND MALARIA

▶ Worldwide, up to 400 million people suffer from malaria. Around 1 million victims die from malaria each year.

▶ A mosquito does not harm the host animal from which it takes a tiny amount of blood. The host is harmed by any disease-producing organisms the mosquito injects with its saliva.

▶ Allergic* reactions to mosquito bite are reactions to substances present in the saliva which act to stimulate the blood flowing and stop it clotting.

▶ The malaria parasite belongs to a group of around 5000 organisms which parasitise animals.

▶ When it enters a red blood cell, a malaria parasite feeds on the haemoglobin (oxygen-carrying substance) it contains.

Christmas Beetles eating eucalypt leaves

49

Spiders, like insects, have exoskeletons and jointed limbs. With scorpions, ticks and mites, they are placed in the class Arachnida – arthropods which have chelicerae* (jaws plus fangs) and lack antennae. Spiders are placed in the order Araneae, for they differ from other arachnids* in having abdominal glands which produce silk. There are two main groups of Australian spiders:

"Primitive" spiders (Mygalomorphs) take in air through two pairs of abdominal pouches filled with gill-like leaves, called book-lungs. They have chelicerae which work up and down, and usually two pairs of spinnerets, which feed out silk from the abdomen.

"True" or "modern" spiders (Araneomorphs) take in air through one pair of book-lungs as well as through tracheal tubes. Their chelicerae work side to side, and they have three pairs of spinnerets and a spinning-plate called a cribellum* (which some groups have lost).

Classification of Red-back Spider
Latrodectus hasselti

Kingdom: Animalia   **Family:** Theridiidae
Phylum: Arthropoda   **Genus:** *Latrodectus*
Class: Arachnida   **Species:** *L. hasselti*
Order: Araneae

Pickaxes to pincers

The spiders which existed around 300 million years ago were bulky, had chelicerae which worked up and down, like pick-axes, and lived in burrows. They breathed through book-lungs and used silk to line burrows and spin egg sacs. Today's "primitive" funnel-web spiders, trapdoor spiders and brush-footed spiders resemble these ancestors.

By 245 million years ago, one group of spiders had developed a cribellum on the abdomen, and combs on the fourth pair of legs for manipulating silk leaving the cribellum. Their chelicerae closed from side to side, they breathed through book-lungs and tracheae and used silk for homes and snares. Today's active hunters and orb web weavers are descended from this group.

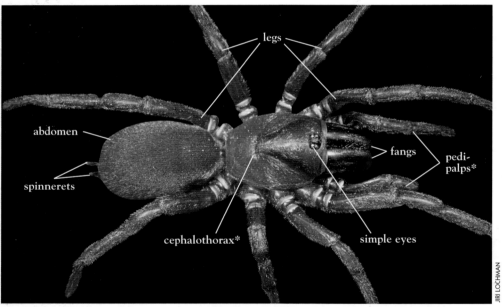

Above: Top view of a trapdoor spider. Below: Diagrammatic section of a spider's body

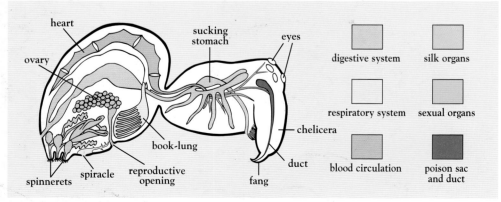

digestive system   silk organs

respiratory system   sexual organs

blood circulation   poison sac and duct

JIRI LOCHMAN

Head-on view of huntsman spider, showing sideways-closing chelicerae, pedipalps and eight simple eyes (set in two lines, four smaller eyes over four larger ones)

WADE HUGHES

Wolf spider, showing fangs and six eyes (two more are set back on the cephalothorax)

IS IT A SPIDER OR IS IT AN INSECT?

SPIDER

- Body divided into two sections, with a waist between.
- Four pairs of walking legs.
- Usually six to eight simple eyes.
- Lack antennae and wings.
- Abdomen bears silk glands, which open on spinnerets.
- Lack true jaws. Feed by injecting poison, pouring on digestive juices which break down tissues, then sucking up liquid by action of "sucking stomach".

INSECT

- Body divided into three sections (not always obvious).
- Three pairs of walking legs.
- Simple and compound eyes.
- Have antennae and often wings.
- Abdomen lacks silk glands and spinnerets.
- Have true jaws, adapted for various ways of eating. Some insects, e.g., flies, dissolve food with digestive juices, then suck up resulting fluid.

D. KNOWLES

A jumping spider which mimics an ant

JIRI LOCHMAN

A jumping ant

FACTS

▶ In an ancient myth, Arachne was a Greek woman who challenged the goddess Athena to a weaving contest. She was changed into a spider and doomed to spin and weave for ever afterwards. Hence the name Arachnida for the class to which spiders belong.

▶ Worldwide, there are about 25 300 species of spiders so far named.

▶ The earliest fossil of a spider discovered so far lived over 360 million years ago.

▶ Australia's oldest spider fossils, found in South Gippsland, Vic., have been dated to over 120 million years ago.

The bluish-white, sticky silk of the Black House Spider is produced through a cribellum, or spinning plate

A wolf spider waits at the entrance to its silk-lined burrow

Silk, the secret of success

One major reason for the success of spiders is the silk they produce and the ways in which they use it.

Spider silk is mainly made up of proteins*. It leaves the spider's body as a liquid which hardens rapidly in the air, then does not dissolve in water. It is very strong, and can stretch to add one-third more to its length, then snap back to its original length without change in shape.

Silk is produced in glands which make up a large part of a spider's abdomen. Different glands make different sorts of silk to be used for purposes including the manufacture of egg sacs, lining shelters and constructing webs. Silk is also used for the safety lines many spiders drag behind them, which save them if they fall. Young spiders spin silken threads on which they "balloon" through the air.

Many tiny tubes connect each silk gland with a spinneret. The sticky fluid which coats the strands in orb webs and catching lines is applied in these tubes.

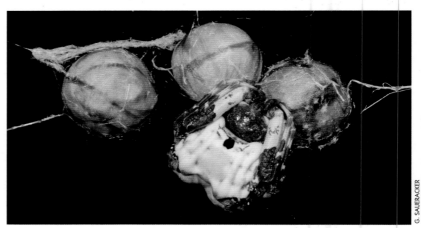

Spiders wrap their eggs in tough cases made of special silk

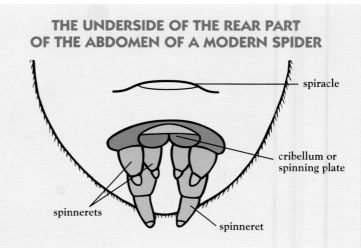

THE UNDERSIDE OF THE REAR PART OF THE ABDOMEN OF A MODERN SPIDER

spiracle

cribellum or spinning plate

spinnerets

spinneret

A male Peacock Jumping Spider courting a female

A female wolf spider carrying young spiders

Mate, not dinner

A female spider is often much larger than a male of the same species, and is sometimes quite different in appearance. Courtship is lengthy, for the male must convince the female he is a mate and not prey.

To introduce himself, a male may posture, dance, pluck a female's web or present gift-wrapped prey. He spins a special web, expels sperm onto it, then sucks the sperm into bulbs on the ends of his pedipalps. When he judges it is safe to do so, he inserts the end of a pedipalp into the female's reproductive opening and discharges the sperm it carries.

The female stores the sperm until she is ready to lay eggs. She may lay 100 at a time, protecting them in a silken egg sac.

Sacs and tiny spiders

Silken egg sacs may be hidden in vegetation, or in crevices, or buried in the ground. Most are guarded. The sacs may be carried around on the spinnerets, between the legs or in the jaws. Female wolf spiders may allow young to climb on their backs and transport them.

A long-jawed spider which mimics a green ant

Camouflage

A wraparound spider from the Great Sandy Desert resting on a twig

Spiders may rely on camouflage to protect them from predators such as birds. They may blend in with the colour or texture of their background in order to lie in ambush waiting for their own prey. A wraparound spider has a broad abdomen which is so flattened that the spider can wrap itself around a twig. Bird-dropping spiders and crab spiders are also well camouflaged by colour and texture. Some spiders mimic insects such as ants.

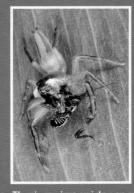
The jumping spider seen here with its cockroach prey is green, and hides on green leaves

Fangs like pick-axes

FACTS

▶ A primitive spider raises its cephalothorax in order to give the chelicerae room to swing downwards.

▶ The poison glands of primitive spiders are located in the bases of the chelicerae and not in the head, as in modern spiders.

▶ Primitive spiders have poor eyesight and usually hunt after dark. They crush their prey with their chelicerae and inject venom*.

▶ The primitive spiders take several years to mature. A female may live 20 years.

▶ If a female spider eats a male after mating, she boosts her protein intake before egg-laying.

▶ Twelve species of trapdoor spiders were found in a 6 km walk across the Lamington Plateau, Qld.

This trapdoor spider's burrow is in a habitat which suits primitive spiders, the damp rainforest

A primitive spider uses its pedipalps to investigate objects

The underside of a trapdoor spider, showing the openings to its two pairs of book-lungs. This spider is shamming death

"Primitive" spiders, or Mygalomorphs, include the most venomous and largest Australian species.

They are large spiders with huge chelicerae, which move up and down rather than from side to side, and eight eyes. Each of the first pair of legs bears a double row of spines. Males of some species have spurs or knobs, which are used in mating, on the second pair of legs. Primitive spiders breathe through book-lungs, have no tracheae and live in cool burrows or in silk tubes.

Among Australia's primitive spiders are the mouse spiders, the trapdoor spiders, the funnel-web spiders, and the brush-footed trapdoor spiders.

A perilous courtship

A newly mature male primitive spider leaves his burrow forever, to wander in search of females. If the female he finds has not already mated, and has recently eaten, he may be allowed to evade her chelicerae, then bend his pedipalps one by one under her body to deposit his sperm. He may survive the encounter, but will die much sooner than his mate.

Mouse spiders

Australia has eight species of mouse spider. Stoutly built trapdoor spiders with huge chelicerae, they may measure up to 35 mm in body length. The brightly coloured male of one species is so different from the female that for many years, until a pair was discovered mating, they were thought to be two distinct species.

The female mouse spider is dull coloured compared to the male

A HOME WITH A DOOR

A trapdoor spider's burrow with the lid closed

A spider waiting inside the burrow

A trapdoor spider's burrow plugged for breeding

The burrow is lined with silk

FACTS

▶ A trapdoor spider may hold its burrow lid closed with a force equal to 140 times the spider's own weight.

▶ Trapdoor spiders developed in warm, damp tropical jungles. Some Australian species now live in arid country, but the male only leaves his burrow to search for females in humid weather.

▶ Predators on trapdoor spiders include wasps, bandicoots, scorpions and centipedes.

▶ Some trapdoor spiders dig burrows using rows of spines on the chelicerae, aided by their front pairs of legs. Others use the legs only. Grains of earth brought up by the chelicerae are flicked away by the pedipalps.

▶ The door or lid of a burrow is made of earth pellets held in place with silk.

Trapdoor spiders

Trapdoor spiders are not generally considered dangerous to humans, though the aggressive female mouse spiders (see p. 54) have large fangs and high venom output and may harm humans. Most trapdoor spiders can be told from funnel-web spiders, which are highly dangerous, by their brown or mottled colours (funnel-webs are usually black and lack markings). When in danger, a trapdoor spider will "freeze" or flee, while a funnel-web will rear back aggressively.

A trapdoor spider may live in a silk tube woven under a stone, a log or bark. The tube may have a door. Some trapdoor spiders dig shafts more than a metre deep. The walls may be plastered with mud and digestive juices, then lined with silk. The spider constructs a lid to close the entrance. Some lids fit tightly; others are simple flaps that open on strong silk hinges. If the lid is tested by an invader, the spider may hold it down with claws and fangs. A trapdoor spider may dig a false passage to fool predators, or an extra exit through which to evade them.

Prey's eye view of a trapdoor spider

DID YOU KNOW?

FACTS

▶ If you were foolish enough to let a brush-footed spider run up your arm, you would later discover tiny red marks where the "toothed" hairs on the spider's feet clung to your skin.

▶ When a brush-footed trapdoor spider is submerged, its hairy body holds air bubbles. This air "pocket" keeps the spider from drowning.

▶ Young brush-footed trapdoor spiders stay in the burrow with their mother for some time.

▶ Brush-footed spiders are also known as bird-eating spiders. One was seen to eat a baby domestic chicken.

A brush-footed trapdoor spider from the Kimberley Division, WA

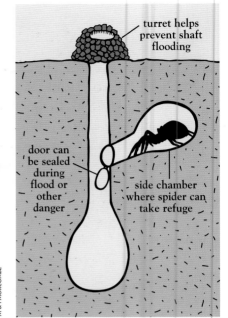

turret helps prevent shaft flooding

door can be sealed during flood or other danger

side chamber where spider can take refuge

Brush-footed trapdoor spider burrow

Hooks on their feet

The brush-footed trapdoor spiders have tufts of "tooth-ended" hairs on their feet which allow them to climb smooth, vertical shafts.

One group digs burrows in ground which is liable to flood. A turret built around the entrance keeps out water and if the burrow is flooded the spider retreats to a side chamber to try to survive until the water recedes.

Another group makes whistling sounds by rubbing flattened pegs on the pedipalps across spines at the bases of the chelicerae. This whistling probably attracts mates.

A brush-footed trapdoor spider on its turret

A brush-footed trapdoor spider from Cape York and an adult finger

HOW THE "WHISTLING SPIDER" WHISTLES

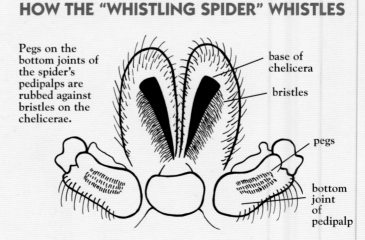

Pegs on the bottom joints of the spider's pedipalps are rubbed against bristles on the chelicerae.

base of chelicera

bristles

pegs

bottom joint of pedipalp

The deadly funnel-webs

All funnel-web spiders are potentially dangerous to humans and other primates*. Their venom attacks the nerves, causing frenzied twitching and a profuse flow of body fluids. A bitten limb should be immobilised and pressure-bandaged and the victim taken immediately to hospital, where antivenom* will be administered.

The male Sydney Funnel-web is one of the world's most dangerous spiders. During the breeding season, he leaves his burrow and searches for females. When threatened, he will attack rather than retreat. After reaching sexual maturity he does not hunt prey, so his poison sacs contain much more concentrated toxin than those of the female, which hunts constantly and so uses and renews her poison.

Tube, not funnel

A typical funnel-web nest is shaped like a long white silken tube, with a pouch at the end in which the spider hides during day. The tube usually has two entrances, so it forms a Y shape.

The tube is spun in a hole or crevice, and the entrance is surrounded by a webbing of trip-lines which warn the spider of likely prey.

FACTS

▶ The body of a female Sydney Funnel-web measures about 35 mm in length, that of a male about 25 mm.

▶ Only around 15 deaths from funnel-web bites have been recorded in Australia in the past 60 years.

▶ Male funnel-webs look for mates in summer and autumn months.

SPIDERS WHOSE BITES MAY HARM HUMANS

Sydney Funnel-web
Blue Mountains Funnel-web
Northern Tree Funnel-web
White-tailed Spider
Mouse Spider
Black House Spider
Red-back Spider
Some wolf spiders

Juvenile White-tailed Spider

D. KNOWLES

D. KNOWLES

A funnel-web spider hunting at night

PAVEL GERMAN

A Sydney Funnel-web ready to attack

PAVEL GERMAN

Sydney Funnel-web in a calmer mood

57

Pursuers and pouncers

FACTS

▶ Huntsman spiders originally lived in woodlands and forests. Today, they often take up residence on the walls of houses, hunting insects at nights. Most are harmless to humans but their chalky droppings may offend the houseproud.

▶ Male and female huntsman spiders have a lengthy courtship, which involves mutual caresses. The male is rarely attacked.

▶ A female huntsman spider places her egg sac under bark or rock, then stands guard. She tears open the egg-sac to help the spiderlings emerge and stays with them for several weeks.

▶ Huntsman spiders may be found huddled together in family groups under flaking bark or rock.

This huntsman spider has just moulted its old skin, which clings to the bark

The "modern spiders" breathe through tracheae as well as through book-lungs. They also have chelicerae which close side-to-side. Groups of modern spiders catch prey in different ways. Pages 58–61 of this book are devoted to keen-eyed spiders which see prey, then catch and eat it.

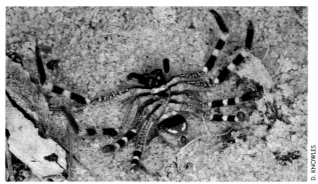

A threatened huntsman spider "plays dead"

A female huntsman guarding her egg sac

Runs like a crab

The legs of a huntsman spider fan out sideways and the joints bend forwards. This means these spiders can run sideways as well as forwards – useful under bark and among stones.

A huntsman spider can move sideways crab-fashion

Huntsman spider with katydid

A burrowing wolf spider leaving home

Wolves on eight legs

Wolf spiders are pursuers which live on the ground, many "denning" in burrows. These are long-legged spiders, whose cephalothoraxes often carry radiating markings. They breathe through one pair of book-lungs and tracheae and hunt by spotting prey with their keen eyes, stalking it, then running it down.

Some species of wolf spiders dig a burrow up to 25 centimetres deep with their jaws, even in hard ground. They spread the debris away from the opening. A silk fence keeps water out of the entrance. Some wolf spiders make doors from silk camouflaged with animal droppings.

The bites of some types of wolf spiders may cause ulcers in human tissue.

FACTS

▶ A male wolf spider courts a female by waving his pedipalps and front legs.

▶ The female wolf spider drags her egg sac around. If a burrower, she guards the egg sac in her burrow.

▶ Hatchling wolf spiders crawl onto their mother's body, three to four deep, clinging onto special knob-ended hairs. Many will fall off and perish.

▶ When two mother wolf spiders meet, they may fight. The victor eats the vanquished, then allows the young the other spider was carrying to climb onto her. She will carry them around with her own young for up to six months.

A wolf spider with a meat ant. Note pincer-like chelicerae

A female wolf spider guarding her egg sac

A spider-hunting wasp attacking a wolf spider

A female wolf spider hunting with a cargo of young spiders

59

DID YOU KNOW?

FACTS

▶ Selenops is related to the huntsman spiders. It has 6 eyes, its legs and body are speckled and it is so flattened that it looks like a cardboard cut-out. It is found under bark and stones.

Female White-tailed Spider

▶ The White-tailed Spider builds a silken cell in which to rest. At night, it may enter another spider's web and twitch a strand. When the web owner rushes out looking for a captured insect, it is eaten.

▶ The female White-tailed Spider may grow to 20 mm in body length, the more slender male to 12 mm. Bacterial infection from a bite from this species can cause an ulcer which may take some time to heal.

Selenops has very long and elegantly striped legs

Lynx spiders are camouflaged in foliage and flower colours

Pounce like a lynx

Lynx spiders live amongst foliage, where they stalk their prey then pounce upon it, sometimes leaping quite a distance. They have long, slender legs covered with long, sharp spines. When the wind sways the leaves, a lynx spider sways back and forth on its long legs. These spiders make no homes: their egg sacs lie in bundles of leaves tied together loosely with silk.

Walking on water

Water spiders frequent fresh or brackish water, running across the surface, feeding on floating insects. If they break the surface and fall in, air trapped in hairs on the abdomen allows them to breathe under water. The female makes a "nursery" shelter for her egg sac.

A water spider can run across the surface of water

A jumping spider hunts during the day. It has an all-round view of its surroundings and it can detect movement up to 20 cm away with its large central front eyes. It stalks the quarry, fastens a safety line, then leaps onto its victim, seizing it as seen here.

FACTS
ABOUT
JUMPING SPIDERS

▶ Australia has about 250 species of jumping spiders.

▶ Tufts of hairs behind their claws give jumping spiders non-skid footing.

▶ A male jumping spider courts a female by "dancing" to display any special markings. Peacock Spider males (top photo, right hand column) have particularly colourful abdomens.

▶ A jumping spider may "high jump" 20 cm or more and can leap 25 times its own body length. Its trailing silken safety line keeps it stable in flight as well as checking it if it falls.

▶ The male of one jumping spider, the Gliding Spider, can extend hair-fringed flaps from the sides of its abdomen. These help it "glide" while leaping.

▶ Spider-hunting wasps may stock their cells with jumping spiders as food for their larvae. On average, a cell will hold ten spiders.

Lurkers and lure-casters

DID YOU KNOW?

These spiders use silk in various ways. Some may weave lacy webs to take prey, or construct silken shelters for themselves and sometimes for their egg sacs. They may snare prey with the aid of a silken net or "fishing line", then truss it in silk. They may lurk in hiding, depending on silken trip-lines to alert them when prey appears. They usually live above ground level, often in foliage, and some are patterned and coloured to resemble their usual surroundings.

Red-back Spider - only the female's fangs can pierce human skin

JIRI LOCHMAN

Deadly Red-back

Bites from female Red-back Spiders killed only around one dozen Australians between 1927, when records were first kept, and 1956, when an antivenom became available. There have been no deaths since.

A Red-back Spider has combs of spines on its hindlegs. These spines are used to spread the silk as it leaves the spinnerets while prey is being wrapped. Members of this species usually build their tangled, "gum-footed" webs close to the ground and may be found around homes and out-buildings.

DID YOU KNOW?

FACTS

▶ Australia's Red-back Spider is related to the American Black Widow and the NZ Katipo, both creatures of popular legend.

▶ The Black House Spider favours the corners of windows. The female, which may grow to 18 mm body length, builds a funnel-shaped, lacy web.

▶ The strands of a Black House Spider's web are woolly and entangle bristles on an insect's body. The vibrations from its struggle are picked up by sensitive hairs on the spider's legs.

JIRI LOCHMAN

Female Black House Spider

▶ A bite from a Black House Spider is not deadly to humans, though it may cause pain and vomiting.

THE GUM-FOOTED WEB OF A COMB-FOOTED SPIDER

spider in refuge

taut threads with sticky beads fastened to surface below web

When an insect contacts the threads below the web, it sticks to the gummy blobs. The thread often breaks at ground level, leaving the insect suspended until the spider arrives.

M & I MORCOMBE

Nicademus bicolor poses no threat to humans

Colourful but harmless

The brilliantly coloured *Nicademus bicolor*, which lives on the underside of its sheet web, is related to the Red-back, but is not dangerous. Perhaps predators leave it alone because of its resemblance to the deadlier species.

Fishing for food

A net-casting spider makes a rectangular framework of dry silk, then fills in the "net" with adhesive silk teased into tiny coils with its hindlegs. This net is very strong, and can stretch up to ten times its original size.

The spider hangs head downwards, net held in its first two pairs of legs. When an insect comes into range, it is netted, wrapped in the net and bitten.

When a net-casting spider has caught its prey, it may eat its net for a quick protein boost as it weaves a new net. It hunts at night. During the daytime, it looks like a dry twig.

A net-casting spider waiting to snare prey

FACTS

▶ A net-casting spider's net is about the size of a small postage stamp.

▶ The scents given out by a Bolas Spider attract different sorts of moth at different times of year.

▶ Some net-casting spiders are called ogre-faced spiders, because of their staring eyes.

The female Bolas* Spider hangs from a horizontal silk thread, dangling a sticky silk line from a front leg. She gives out a scent which attracts male moths, who are lured close enough to be hit and tangled by the swung line. The moth is then played like a hooked fish until it can be reeled in and bitten.

Ogre-faced spider

63

▶ Australia has about 9 species of triangular spiders, which ambush insects, seizing them with their spiky forelegs.

▶ Triangular spiders are found in eucalypts, and favour areas of regrowth after bushfires. Here, their vivid colours blend with the colours of regenerating bark and leaves.

Crab spiders

The two front pairs of legs of a crab spider are long, strong and spiny. All four pairs of legs can be fanned sideways so the spider can flatten itself against leaf or branch. Eight eyes, often raised on tiny turrets, give a 360° field of vision.

Some crab spiders are textured and coloured to resemble bark or lichen. The cuticle is often bare of hairs, and may be shiny. These spiders sit with legs drawn up and wait until a victim moves within range, then seize it with the long front legs.

Crab spiders do not build a web, though they may be found dangling from a single strand of silk at night. The leaf-curling crab spider builds a retreat, or an egg-sac shelter, by folding over the tip of a leaf or a blade of grass to form a tent and fastening it with silk.

Crab spider and wasp prey

Female bird-dropping spider guarding egg sacs

Following the scent

Bird-dropping spiders have leathery bodies coloured black, brown and white to resemble birds' droppings. A young bird-dropping spider builds a small wheel web, but an adult lures moths by sending out odours the insects find attractive, then pouncing when they fly close.

A platform spider builds a sheet-web over water

Triangular spiders from the southwest of Western Australia

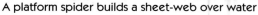

A flower spider with a fly

A flower spider guarding the egg-sac

A flower spider waiting for prey

A flower spider with prey, an Evening Brown Butterfly

DEATH IN PETALS

Flower spiders are often white or yellow in colour; some have green, brown or rosy tints on the abdomen. Each spider takes a flower as its hunting territory and waits in the petals, anchored by its hind legs, with its front legs and pedipalps extended. An insect visiting the flower for pollen or nectar is seized and bitten, then sucked dry.

Artists in silk

An orb web and its builder

The wheel-shaped orb web is the ultimate use of silk to trap prey, especially when woven where flying insects abound. There are many different types of orb webs.

When a victim blunders into the web, it is snared by the sticky threads. Alerted by the vibrations caused by its struggles, the spider quickly trusses it in silk, preventing it tearing the web. It then injects venom into the victim and sucks out its juices. A male orb web spider may announce his identity to a female by plucking strands of her web.

DID YOU KNOW?

FACTS

▶ When a spider moves on its web, it holds the sticky silk with claw-like bristles on the ends of its legs. If it is knocked onto the web, oil on its body prevents it sticking to the strands.

▶ Some orb webs are complete circles, others are incomplete. Some species, like the St Andrews Cross Spider, weave extra stabilising threads into their webs.

▶ In space, on a shuttle, two orb web spiders made unnaturally perfect webs in the absence of gravity.

▶ Moths are caught in orb webs less frequently than other insects. Scales on their bodies prevent the web sticking.

Dew adheres to the sticky spiral threads of a spider's web

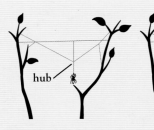

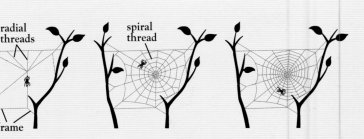

1. The spider pays out a silk thread which the wind carries to a second anchor point. This bridge is strengthened by additional silk threads passed back and forth across it. Then the spider makes a Y shape which becomes the first three radial threads.

2. The bottom of the stem of the Y is anchored to the ground or another firm object. A frame is constructed and radial threads are attached to surrounding objects.

3. The spider makes a "safe track", or scaffolding, of non-sticky silk, working from the centre to the edge of the web.

4. The spider then works back to the centre of the web, removing the dry silk and replacing it with sticky silk. The sticky silk is tied to each radial thread, then plucked to twang the gum into regular sticky beads.

BUILDING AN ORB WEB

A garden spider hiding during daytime

... and on her web at night, ready to seize prey

This Golden Orb-weaver's web has caught a skink

Wheels of gold

Female Golden Orb-weaver Spiders are large (up to 45 mm body length), but males are tiny (only about 6 mm in length).

These spiders often live in gardens and are harmless to humans. A female's web, made of strong golden silk, may measure one metre across and is inhabited by the owner day and night. A large web may snare a small bird or even a bat; any damage is promptly repaired.

FACTS

▶ The Golden Orb-weaver makes a tangled barrier of threads in front of and behind the orb web.

▶ Many small spiders such as Dewdrop Spiders live on a Golden Orb-weaver's web, eating prey too small for the owner.

▶ The "cross" on which the St Andrews Cross Spider rests adds strength to the web.

▶ When disturbed, the female St Andrews Cross Spider grasps her web and shakes it vigorously.

▶ Wraparound spiders have broad, flat abdomens. They remain hiding during day and spin orb webs to catch insects at night.

The underside of a Golden Orb-weaver

St Andrews Cross Spider is harmless to humans

The turret on the abdomen of this wraparound spider looks like the broken-off base of a twig

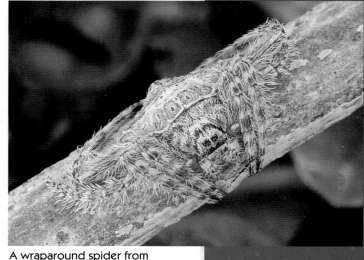
A wraparound spider from central Australia

67

DID YOU KNOW?

FACTS

▶ In spite of long-jawed spiders' fearsome fangs, they are harmless to humans.

▶ A Two-spined Spider dismantles and usually eats her web at daybreak, then hides under leaves until it is time to spin another web late next night.

▶ Spiny spiders, which include Christmas and Jewel Spiders, are harmless to people. They build wheel webs with small, fluffy balls of silk along the strands forming the frame.

▶ The female Two-spined Spider's abdomen changes colour as the spider pumps body fluids into the area.

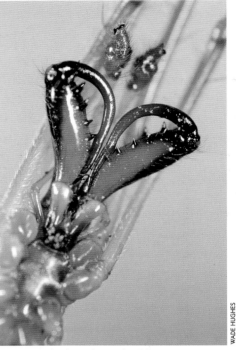

The jaws of a long-jawed spider

A Two-spined Spider

A long-jawed spider in its web

Lock lips with me!

A courting male long-jawed spider meets the female with jaws open. Special "teeth" on his chelicerae lock into her chelicerae, so he can stop her biting him while mating.

Long-jawed spiders are usually found in vegetation along creeks and near swamps. Their horizontal orb webs are often built over the water of streams, swamps and ponds.

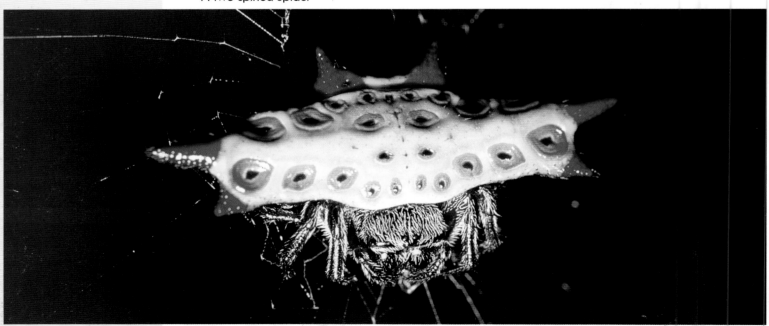

This spiny Jewel Spider has six spikes projecting from around the edges of its broad, armoured abdomen

Tail-stingers and others

A scorpion in defensive posture

Ticks and mites

Ticks and many mites are arachnids which parasitise other animals. Some mites are predators or feed on plant fluids. The abdomen of a tick or mite has no external segments: as with scorpions, there is no "waist" between cephalothorax and abdomen.

A tick feeding on human blood

This scarab beetle carries parasitic mites behind its horn

A scorpion is an arachnid with a long tail which ends in a sting and is held over the body in defensive posture. The pedipalps are large, the last two segments forming grasping pincers. Under the body, behind the legs, is a pair of comb-like structures which are sensitive to chemical traces.

A scorpion feeds on other invertebrates, seizing prey with the pincers and striking it repeatedly with the sting before sucking out its fluids. Human fatalities from scorpion sting have been rare in Australia, though they are more common in other parts of the world.

Shall we waltz?

A male scorpion deposits a stalked spermatophore on the ground. Then he takes the female's pincers in his and dances her around until her reproductive opening is over the packet. She takes it in to fertilise her eggs.

The female gives birth to live young, then carries them on her back for some time before they go off to survive on their own.

A harvestman on a patch of moss

FACTS

▶ Scorpions are found all over Australia. The largest species may be 12 cm in length.

A scorpion's pincers are formed from the final segments of its pedipalps

▶ Under ultra-violet light, a scorpion has a fluorescent shine.

▶ Harvestmen are less than 1 cm in body length but have very long legs. They live in moist leaf litter.

▶ Harvestmen have only one pair of eyes, lack a "waist", do not have silk glands and cannot make silk. They are sometimes called "daddy-long-legs", but should not be confused with the harmless, house-loving, web-dwelling spider of that name.

DID YOU KNOW?

FACTS

▶ Despite their name, which means "100 feet", very few species of centipede have as many as 100 legs. The centipedes on this page have 21 or 23 pairs of legs.

▶ Centipedes may prey on animals as large as frogs, geckos and mice.

▶ In courtship, male and female centipedes tap each other with their antennae. Then the male spins a silk mat onto which he deposits a packet of sperm. The female picks up the offering with her reproductive opening.

▶ A centipede bite may be painful, but is not lethal to humans.

Many legs

Centipedes, house centipedes (which are also called scutigera) and millipedes belong to a group of arthropods with unbranched limbs. Centipedes have one pair of legs to each obvious segment. Millipedes appear to have two pairs of legs to each segment, but closer examination shows that each "segment" is really two fused together. Centipedes eat other animals, while millipedes are generally vegetarian.

A centipede feeding

A centipede in the Northern Territory eating a Freshwater Snake

A Little Red Antechinus (a marsupial which eats small animals) subduing a centipede

The poison's under the head

Underneath its head, each centipede shown here possesses a pair of fangs, which are specialised limbs from the first body segment. These fangs contain the openings to a pair of venom glands.

Venom injected by the fangs kills the prey, which is torn into pieces by the jaws, after which the soft pieces are eaten.

A centipede's final pair of legs are often strong and brightly coloured. They are not venomous or dangerous, but they may be waved in defensive display and are used to grasp prey.

Adult millipedes have two pairs of legs on each apparent body segment. Nine different groups live in Australia. They feed on decaying vegetable matter and are found in moist places, such as under logs. Millipedes lack venom but some groups produce an irritating fluid in self-defence. The millipede above left is feeding, the one above right is coiled up and "playing dead".

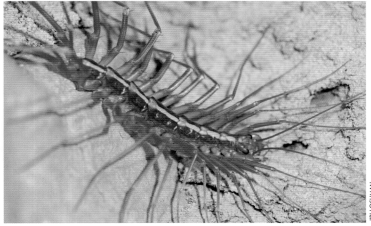

The speedy house centipede is nicknamed "Johnny Hairylegs"

Johnny Hairylegs

The house centipede, or scutigera, has only 15 pairs of legs. It normally lives under rocks or bark, but may enter houses, where it seizes insects or spiders with its legs before killing them with its venomous claws. It is harmless to humans.

HOW ARTHROPODS GAIN STABILITY

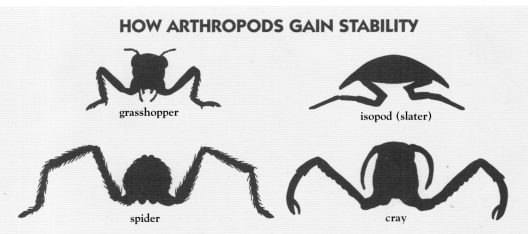

grasshopper

isopod (slater)

spider

cray

Arthropods are too small and light to perch on their legs as mammals do. To give them stability, they hang suspended from their legs or, like the isopods, crouch low over them, so keeping their bodies close to the ground.

FACTS

▶ Male millipedes have special mating legs with which they transfer their sperm into the female's reproductive opening.

▶ Some millipedes protect themselves by rolling up and "playing dead". Others discharge a reddish or yellowish, unpleasant fluid.

▶ An introduced species, the Black Portuguese Millipede, may reach pest proportions in southeastern Australia, invading houses and destroying crops.

▶ A newly emerged young house centipede has only four pairs of legs. Extra pairs are added at each moult.

▶ The end of a house centipede's leg contains several hundred small segments.

▶ A house centipede can reach a speed of half a metre per second. It has only one gait, in which four legs on each side are in contact with the ground at any time.

Armoured wonders

Slaters are land-living crustaceans

Shield shrimps, brine and other shrimps, crabs, crays and slaters all belong to a group of arthropods called the Crustacea.

All crustaceans have bodies divided into head, thorax and abdomen. Many have the thorax protected by a carapace*. They all have two pairs of antennae and many other appendages*, which are used for feeding, walking and swimming.

Brine shrimps normally swim with legs uppermost

Shrimp soup

After good rains, arid central Australia's inland lakes explode into life with countless numbers of tiny brine shrimps and shield shrimps. These form food for the huge numbers of birds which gather to breed near these lakes.

Shield shrimps are small primitive crustaceans. They die when the water dries up, leaving millions of eggs behind in the parched and cracking ground. When rain falls again to fill claypans and lakes, these eggs hatch and begin a new generation of shield shrimps.

Dying shield shrimps on a drying waterhole

Freshwater crabs

Australia has at least seven species of freshwater crabs. The most common one is found across the north of the continent and in the upper reaches of the Darling River system. These crabs survive dry seasons by plugging their burrows with earth. To cope with uncertain climate, the eggs hatch direct into tiny crabs instead of into a free-swimming larval stage.

One of Australia's seven freshwater crab species

Lamington Plateau Cray confronts danger

Marron, Yabby, Gilgie or Lobby?

Australia has over 100 species of freshwater crays, identified by common names such as Marron, Yabby, Gilgie or Lobby. Freshwater crays hatch as miniature adults, not as tiny larvae, as happens with most other crustaceans. This allows them to grow quickly and survive if water becomes scarce.

TOP VIEW OF A FRESHWATER CRAY

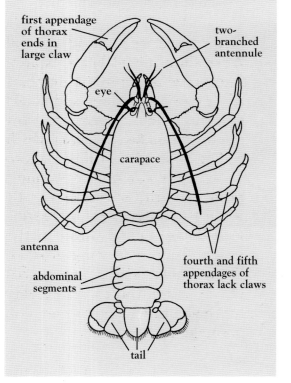

- first appendage of thorax ends in large claw
- two-branched antennule
- eye
- carapace
- antenna
- abdominal segments
- fourth and fifth appendages of thorax lack claws
- tail

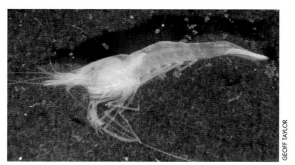
A blind cave shrimp from northwest Australia

A freshwater prawn, or Cherabin

The Marron, one of the world's largest freshwater crays

A Yabby swimming

73

Soft-bodied slitherers

FACTS

- Australia's native earthworms often disappear after land is cleared. Introduced species take over gardens and pastures.

- Australia's largest earthworm is found in Gippsland, Vic., and may grow to 3 m.

- Earthworms mix surface and sub-surface soil as they burrow. Soil eaten is stripped of food material, then voided as "castings" on the surface.

- Being hermaphrodite is an advantage to animals which live solitary lives. An earthworm can be sure that any other earthworm it meets is of the opposite sex.

- Earthworms mate for 3–4 hours. During this period, each keeps its tail in its burrow, ready to retreat if necessary.

- Flatworms, which have flattened bodies, include free-living scavengers and carnivores, and parasites such as tapeworms and flukes.

- Most free-living flatworms are 2–3 cm long, though some may grow to 30 cm.

Southern Brown Bandicoot eating an earthworm

Earthworms and leeches have long, cylinder-shaped bodies made up of many fairly similar segments. They have no appendages or antennae. Leeches differ from earthworms by having suckers on both ends and by feeding on blood. Flatworms have soft, flattened bodies covered with mucus. Their undersides carry tiny hairs, used to aid movement.

Sperm-swappers

Earthworms are hermaphrodites*, having both male and female sex organs. These open onto the clitellum, a gland-bearing area on the front part of the body.

When earthworms mate, they exchange sperm. Each lays eggs in a cocoon, which is shed and lies in the soil until the young hatch.

A giant earthworm from the North Qld rainforest

EARTHWORMS AFTER MATING

Eggs pass from the female opening into a cocoon produced by the clitellum. Then the worm wriggles backwards.

As the cocoon passes over the stored sperm, the eggs are fertilised.

head

clitellum

female reproductive opening

male reproductive openings eject sperm

sperm received and stored here

clitellum

head

female reproductive opening

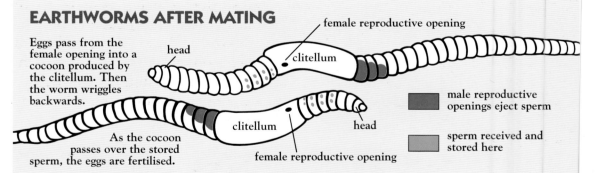

Free-living flatworms live under logs or bark or in other moist situations

74

BLOOD-SUCKERS OF THE FORESTS

PETER MARSACK

A leech waiting on foliage for a host

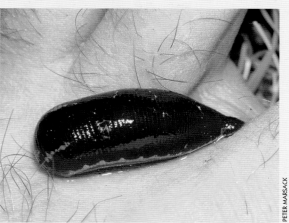

PETER MARSACK

A leech which has fed well on human blood

Leeches feed on blood. A leech waits on foliage or loops over the forest floor, moving towards a possible host with the help of suckers on both ends. It slits the host's skin with its three jaws, then pumps in digestive fluids, which act as pain-killers and prevent the blood clotting as it is sucked up.

PETER MARSACK

Male and female velvet worms

Velvety predators

Velvet worms have skin covered with tiny bumps, giving them a velvety appearance. Most Australian species have 14 to 16 pairs of legs. They capture prey by snaring it in sticky fluid from glands on either side of the mouth, then tearing a hole in it with two pairs of jaws and sucking its body juices.

FACTS

▶ Leeches are hermaphrodites. Sperm may be transferred by a penis, or by injecting it through the body wall.

▶ The pain-killer applied by a leech is so effective that it can feed for a long time without being noticed by the host.

▶ Leeches are still used to control excess blood accumulating after surgery.

▶ Velvet worms are more closely related to arthropods than to worms. Their earliest ancestors existed in the Cambrian period.

▶ A male velvet worm deposits sperm on the female's body. The sperm travels through the body wall to the body cavity, then to the ovaries*.

PETER MARSACK

A velvet worm catching prey in sticky fluid

PETER MARSACK

A velvet worm and young one

Slime-gliders

FACTS

▶ Snails and slugs are gastropods. The word means "stomach foot" and describes the way in which the body and internal organs of such an animal have been twisted back so the stomach lies above the large fleshy foot.

▶ The shell of a snail grows in a coil around its body.

▶ With a shell to protect its body and prevent it from drying out, a snail can venture into various environments.

A snail leaves a trail of dried mucus, or "slime"

▶ When a snail pulls back into its shell, it can close the entrance with mucus, which dries to let air, but not water, through. Some snails fasten themselves firmly to stone, bark or some other surface, preventing moisture escaping from their bodies.

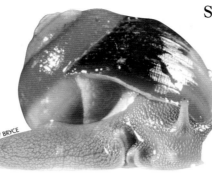

CLAY BRYCE

Slugs and snails belong to a group called molluscs, which includes more than 100 000 species of living animals. Molluscs come in many different forms: gastropods* such as snails and slugs, bivalves* such as oysters, and other creatures such as chitons and octopuses. Most molluscs are aquatic. Those that live on land have developed special ways in which to prevent their bodies drying out.

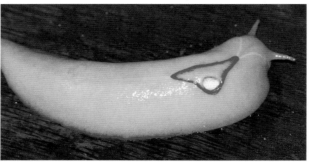

PETER SLATER

This native rainforest slug breathes through a hole on its back signposted by a pink triangle

Track them down

A slug or a snail glides along, powered by surges of wave-like muscle contractions in the under surface of its fleshy foot. These begin at the rear of the foot and pass to the front. Glands under the foot produce mucus, or slime, which makes progress easier and helps the animal cling to sloping surfaces. Snail trails are marked by dried slime. The native slug above leaves a zigzag trail of cleaned surface where it has grazed on simple plants growing on the surface of bark or wood.

Stomach-feet and file-tongues

A gastropod mollusc has a flattened, asymmetrical* body with a head at the front end. Beneath the body is a "foot", a gliding surface kept moist by mucus, and inside is a mass of organs.

Above these organs is a cavity which opens backwards, covered by a fold of the body wall called the mantle. This mantle cavity contains gills or, in the case of land molluscs, has become a lung. The mantle produces a protective shell, which in some molluscs may extend to cover or enclose the body.

All gastropods feed by using a radula, a tongue-like structure covered by rows of rasping teeth.

JIRI LOCHMAN

A slug from temperate rainforest has an obvious mantle

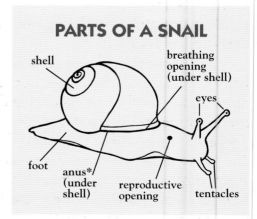

PARTS OF A SNAIL

shell

breathing opening (under shell)

eyes

foot

anus* (under shell)

reproductive opening

tentacles

A land snail from northwestern WA

A land snail from the Top End of the NT

Snail colours

In many places in the world, species of land snail living in a particular environment may be quite differently coloured from the same species living in another habitat. However, Australian native snails are usually found only in one habitat. A species is adapted to live in rainforest, woodland or desert and varies little in colour.

Freshwater snail shells on shore of inland lake

Common Mediterranean Garden Snails mating

Common Garden Snail with eggs

Love darts

Snails and slugs are hermaphrodites. The courtship of the introduced Common Garden Snail involves the partners firing chalky, slightly curved, four-bladed "love darts" at each other.

The missiles, each about 5 mm long, are kept in muscular sacs. The impact of the darts stimulates the mating urge and a pair of snails may spend half a day exchanging long packets of sperm. Inside the snail the walls of the spermatophore are digested and the sperm stored. Each snail later lays eggs in a hole or other protected area; the Common Garden Snail lays between 50 and 100.

Unique and vulnerable

Many of the small, isolated patches of rainforest in the Kimberley Division of Western Australia have their own species of land snail. If a patch of forest burns, or is destroyed, a species may disappear.

FACTS

▶ A slug may lose up to 16% of its body water in an hour by evaporation and the production of mucus. It obtains water through its skin and by eating juicy plants.

▶ A land snail may aestivate to wait out a hot dry period. It withdraws into its shell, conserves water by blocking off the opening into its shell with dried mucus, and becomes inactive.

▶ In very cold weather, the Common Garden Snail may hibernate. Its body functions slow right down and it activates an "anti-freeze" in its blood.

Land snail shells from patches of Kimberley rainforest

Interwoven lives

STEVE PARISH

Biodiversity at work

There are five generally recognised kingdoms of living things – bacteria, fungi, plants, single-celled animals and many-celled animals. Almost anywhere you go on Earth there will be representatives of these kingdoms. In Australia, even on the snowbound top of Mount Kosciusko or in the most sunbaked fastnesses of the central deserts, there will be plants, animals, fungi and bacteria living and reproducing their kind.

The different forms that all of these living organisms take and the different ways in which they live are summed up in the term "biological diversity", or "biodiversity" for convenience.

Whenever you look around you, whether you are in the rainforest or in your garden, you are seeing a scene of enormous biodiversity. In the rainforest, the animal lifeforms range from the huge flightless cassowary down to minute leaf-litter creatures. In your garden the range will be just as extreme, but the numbers of species and of individuals will be less. However, in both places, as anywhere in the world, some creatures feed on plants, some creatures eat other animals, plants feed on the substances which become available when animals and other plants die, and parasites feed on living hosts. Remove any species from its niche in the landscape and the odds are that some other species will either decline sharply or multiply unchecked. Exterminate any species and the world will have lost an irreplaceable resource.

Kill and overkill

The invertebrates which form the subject of this book make up the largest part of the animal kingdom. There are numbers of them which are seen as harmful to human interests in some way – locusts, weevils, caterpillars, mosquitoes, mites, bed-bugs, fleas, ticks, parasitic worms, leeches, cockroaches, scorpions, potentially lethal spiders – plus many more!

Human efforts to get rid of these perceived nuisances using chemicals may be counter-productive. The initial "kill" often leads to resistant strains of the target species, and there is always danger to other living organisms, including humans, from the effects of pesticides. Sometimes the harmful effects of these substances are not apparent for many years.

Biological controls seem to be the safest and surest answer.

Whatever methods are used to control pests, the ultimate effects on the web of life should be a prime concern for all of us.

Endangered butterflies

There are few people who do not enjoy the beauty and grace of butterflies and most find their dramatic life histories fascinating. Some butterfly species are still common in Australia, but others are becoming fewer in numbers. The greatest threat to rarer species is the destruction of their habitat. Some butterfly caterpillars eat only one species of plant, which may be found in a restricted area such as rainforest or sandplain heath. If the larval host plant disappears as the area in which it grows is cleared for development, the butterfly will disappear as well.

STANLEY BREEDEN

Glossary

alates. Winged individuals.

allergic. Unusually sensitive to a substance.

amphibians. Four-limbed vertebrates with moist skins, which usually have water-dwelling immature stage.

amplified. Increased in loudness.

antennae (singular **antenna**). Slender, sensitive feelers found on the heads of all arthropods except arachnids.

antivenom. Substance which combats the action of a venom.

anus. Final opening of digestive canal of animal.

appendages. Things attached; used of limbs of arthropods.

arachnids. Eight-legged arthropods which have simple eyes, sensory pedipalps, pincer-like jaws and which eat fluids only.

asexually. Without male and female sex cells involved.

asymmetrical. Cannot be divided into two or more similar parts by a point, a line, or radiating lines.

bacteria. Microscopic one-celled organisms, some of which cause disease.

biological controls. Predators or parasites used to control plant or animal pests.

bivalves. Molluscs which have two shells, e.g., mussels.

bolas. Missile consisting of balls connected by cord.

camouflage. Colour and pattern which blends with background and makes animal less visible to predators.

carapace. Shield-like plate covering top and sides of the head and thorax of a crustacean.

castes. Different forms of mature social insects.

cellulose. Material making up cell walls of green plants.

cephalothorax. Combined head and thorax.

chelicerae (singular **chelicera**). Arthropod jaws which bear fangs.

colonies. Groups of animals of the same species living closely together.

compound eyes. An eye made up of many image-forming elements.

cribellum. Plate-like spinning organ situated just in front of the spinnerets in some spiders.

crop. Expanded part of digestive tract in which food is stored and/or digested.

cuticle. Dead layer of outermost skin of many invertebrates.

echinoderms. Animals with a skeleton of plates and spines embedded in the body wall, e.g., sea stars and sea urchins.

elytra. Hard forewings of beetle, which cover and protect membranous hindwings.

exoskeleton. An invertebrate skeleton which forms the outermost covering of the body, supporting and shaping it.

feral. In wild state after escape from domestication.

fertile. Capable of becoming a parent to new individuals.

flex. Bend (especially of joint in limb).

gastropods. Molluscs which have an asymmetrical body, well-developed foot, and one or two pairs of tentacles.

habitat. Specific place where a plant or animal lives.

hermaphrodites. Individuals with both female and male reproductive organs.

infertile. Not capable of becoming a parent.

instar. A stage of growth between moults from egg to adult.

introduced. Having been brought from another country or environment.

iridescence. Shiny colours which change with position.

larva (plural **larvae**; adjective **larval**). Active immature stage of an animal which undergoes several sudden changes before adulthood.

mammals. Class of warm-blooded vertebrates which have hair and suckle young on milk.

mandibles. Jaws; feeding appendages.

moult. Shed exoskeleton to allow increase in size.

nuclei. In living cells, the bodies which contain inheritable factors.

nymph. Immature stage of an insect or arachnid which undergoes a gradual series of changes before adulthood.

ovaries. Female reproductive organs in which eggs are produced.

oviduct. Tube which carries eggs away from ovary.

ovipositors. Structures used to deposit eggs.

parasites (verb **parasitise**; adjective **parasitic**). Animals or plants which live on, or in, other species (the hosts) and take nourishment from them.

pedipalps. Appendages on the cephalothorax of an arachnid, used for sensing and manipulating objects.

penis. Male organ which deposits sperm in female.

phylum. A major division of the animal kingdom.

pigments. Colouring materials.

predator. An animal which kills and eats other animals.

primates. Order of animals including lemurs, monkeys, tarsiers, marmosets, apes and humans.

primitive. Appearing to be the earliest or very early stage of growth or evolution of an animal.

proteins. Complex organic compounds which form part of all living things; essential part of animal food.

pupa (plural **pupae**; adjective **pupal**). Inactive immature stage between larva and adult.

rectum. End part of intestine which opens to outside the body.

scavengers. Animals which feed on dead animals that they have not killed.

sexually. With male and female sex cells involved.

simple eyes. Eyes having only one lens.

social. Living with others.

solitary. Living alone.

specialised. Developed in a special way for a special purpose or environment.

sperm (**spermatozoa**). Male reproductive (sex) cells.

spermatophore. Packet containing sperm.

sterile. Not capable of becoming a parent.

taxonomists. People who describe, identify and name living organisms. **Taxonomy** (adjective **taxonomic**) is the scientific naming/classification of living organisms.

territory. An area over which an animal establishes control and then defends against other animals of the same species.

toxic. Poisonous.

toxins. Poisons of animal or plant origin.

trilobite. A marine arthropod now extinct but abundant in Cambrian to Permian periods.

ultrasound. Extremely high-pitched sound.

unpalatable. Unpleasant-tasting.

venom (adjective **venomous**). Poison produced by an animal such as a snake, bee, scorpion, etc.

Map

RECOMMENDED FURTHER READING

CLYNE, DENSEY, 1969, *A Guide to Australian Spiders.*
Thomas Nelson & Sons, Sydney
DAVIES, VALERIE TODD, 1986, *Australian Spiders.*
Queensland Museum, Brisbane
HADLINGTON, P.W. and JOHNSTON, J.A., 1990.
An Introduction to Australian Insects. NSWUP, Sydney
HARVEY, M.S. and YEN, A.L., 1989. *Worms to Wasps:*
An Illustrated Guide to Australia's Terrestrial Invertebrates.
Oxford University Press Australia, Melbourne
JONES, D. and MORGAN, G., 1994. *A Field Guide to*
Crustaceans of Australian Waters. Reed Books, Sydney
MAIN, BARBARA YORK, 1984. *Spiders.* Collins, Sydney

KNOX, LADIGES and EVANS (eds), 1994. *Biology.*
McGraw-Hill Book Company, Sydney
MACQUITTY, MIRANDA, 1995. *Megabugs:*
The Natural History Book of Insects. Carlton Books, London
NEW, T.R., 1991. *Insects as Predators.* NSWUP, Sydney
SIMON-BRUNET, BERT, 1994. *The Silken Web:*
A Natural History of Australian Spiders. Reed Books, Sydney
THE LIVING AUSTRALIA MAGAZINE, 1994.
Dangerous Australians. Bay Books, Sydney
ZBOROWSKI, PAUL and STORY, ROSS, 1995.
A Field Guide to Insects in Australia. Reed Books, Sydney

PHOTOGRAPHY: Australia's finest nature photographers: Steve Parish, Stanley Breeden, Eric Lindgren, Jiri Lochman and photographers of Jiri Lochman Transparencies, M & I Morcombe, Ian Morris, Peter Slater, Raoul Slater, Belinda Wright. ACKNOWLEDGEMENTS: The author's thanks are due to the staff of the Queensland Museum for their helpful comments on the text, and to Leanne Nobilio of Steve Parish Publishing, whose design talents have contributed so much to this series.

First published in Australia by Steve Parish Publishing Pty Ltd
PO Box 2160 Fortitude Valley BC Queensland 4006
© 1997 Copyright photography, illustration and text Steve Parish Publishing Pty Ltd
ISBN 1-875932-35-6